KEY TO

THIRD YEAR LATIN

(1946 REVISION)

BY

ROBERT J. HENLE, S.J.

LOYOLA PRESS.
Chicago

LOYOLA PRESS.
3441 N. Ashland Avenue
Chicago, Illinois 60657
(800) 621-1008
www.loyolapress.com

ISBN-13: 978-0-8294-1209-3
ISBN-10: 0-8294-1209-3

Printed in the United States of America.
16 Bang 10 9 8 7 6 5 4 3

TABLE OF CONTENTS

INTRODUCTION

This key is intended as an aid to the busy teacher. It should serve to unlock readily and speedily whatever may be difficult or obscure, or what would yield—if one had the time—to closer and more lengthy perusal. A few points in connection with the key and its use merit a word of comment.

1. In the English translations of the Latin readings and exercises the literal meanings of Latin words and sentences are usually given, since the main purpose is to make the Latin text clear rather than to give an example of good style. Occasionally a freer translation is added in parentheses. While it may often be necessary to demand a literal translation first, the final translation accepted by the teacher should always be pure, idiomatic English.

2. In translating English exercises into Latin this key seldom gives more than one version. "You" could often be either singular or plural; "they put" could be present, imperfect, or perfect; "I see" can be translated by three or more verbs. It would have been impossible to give every variant translation, nor would any useful purpose have been served by so doing.

3. The author's purpose in calling for the explanation of italicized constructions in certain exercises is to focus attention on points of syntax requiring drill. For the purposes of the key it was deemed sufficient to give the grammar reference. It is understood that the amount of explanation actually required will depend on what the class needs and is able to do and will be determined by the teacher's judgment.

CICERO'S FIRST ORATION AGAINST CATILINE

1. How far, pray, O Catiline, wilt thou abuse our forbearance? Or how long is that madness of yours to make sport of us? To what lengths will your unbridled effrontery vaunt itself? The guard by night on the Palatine Hill, the watches throughout the city, the terror of the populace, the concourse of all good citizens, this well-fortified meeting place of the Senate, the expressions on the faces of these senators about you—do all of these make not the slightest impression on you? Can you be unaware that all your plans lie exposed? Don't you realize that your conspiracy is already blocked by the knowledge of all these men? Do you suppose that any of us is ignorant of what you did last night and the night before last: where you were, whom you called together, what plans you laid?

2. Alas for the times (in which we live) and the (degeneracy of the national) character! The Senate knows all this, the consul sees it, yet this (wretch) continues to live. Did I say he lives? Nay more, he even comes into the Senate (and) takes part in (discussions of) national policy; with his eye he notes down and points out each and every one of us for assassination. But we—brave men that we are!—think we do enough for the state if we but avoid his rage and weapons. You, O Catiline, ought long ago to have been led to death by order of the consul; on your head should have been visited the curse which you have so long been devising for all of us.

3. Publius Scipio, who was high priest as well as a very eminent man, put to death merely in his capacity as a private citizen Tiberius Gracchus, although the latter was but slightly undermining the national constitution. Is it then possible that we the consuls are going to put up with Catiline, aflame as he is with desire to destroy the whole world with murder and fire? For I pass over those too ancient examples: the fact that Gaius Servilius Ahala with his own hand slew Spurius Maelius, who was attempting a revolution. There was, there was once in this state, I say, such a high type of manhood that brave men checked a dangerous citizen with more severe punishment than the most bitter enemy. We hold against you, Catiline, a severe and weighty decree of the Senate. There is no lack of public deliberation nor of the authorization of this body. We, we consuls—I say it openly—are at fault.

4. Once upon a time the Senate decreed that the consul Lucius Opimius should see to it that the state incur no harm. Not a night intervened. On account of some mere hints of treasonable practices Gaius Gracchus met his death, sprung though he was of a distinguished father, grandfather, and ancestors. Killed too together with his children was Marcus Fulvius, a man of consular rank. By a like decree of the Senate the state was entrusted to the consuls Gaius Marius and Lucius Valerius. Did death and a traitor's doom fail by even one day to overtake Lucius Saturninus, tribune of the people, or the praetor Gaius Servilius? But this is now the twentieth day that we have allowed to grow dull the sharp edge of our senatorial authority. For we possess the same kind of senatorial decree, but it lies buried in the archives like a sword hidden away in its scabbard; and yet according to this decree it was befitting that you, Catiline, should have been put to death at once.

5. But you live, and you live not to lay aside but rather to strengthen your brazenness. Gentlemen of the Senate, I desire to be merciful; I desire not to appear remiss at a period of such grave national crisis; but even now I charge myself with inactivity and criminal negligence. There is in Italy a camp against the Roman people, located in the passes of Etruria. Day by day the number of the enemy grows larger. Yet the commander of that camp and the leader of the enemy you behold within the walls and even in the Senate chamber, daily plotting some internal ruin to the state. If I ordered you to be seized and killed, Catiline, I suppose I would have to fear not that all decent men should say that I had acted too late, but rather that anyone would say that I had acted too cruelly. But for a very good reason I have not yet been induced to do what ought rightly to have been done long ago. Then at last will you be put to death when no one can any longer be found so depraved, so abandoned, so like yourself as not to admit that the deed has been done in full justice.

6. So long as there shall be a single one who dares to defend you, you shall live, and you shall live as you are now living, hemmed in by my many strong guards, that you may have no opportunity for a move against the state. Just as they have done up to the present, so shall countless eyes and ears continue to spy upon you and guard you though you do not perceive it.

What can it be that you are still waiting for, if the darkness of night cannot conceal your wicked gatherings or a private home hold within its walls the voices of your conspiracy—if everything bursts forth and stands fully revealed? Take my advice; change your fell purpose and give up the thought of slaughter and arson. You are hemmed in on all sides; all your plots are clearer to us than the light of day. Just consider a few of the items with me.

7. Do you recall that on October 21 I stated in the Senate that Gaius Manlius, your henchman and the accomplice of your bold scheme, would be in arms on a certain day, and that that day would be October 27? Was I deceived about so vast, so terrible, so unbelievable a project, Catiline, or even (what should cause you much greater surprise) about the very day (appointed)? I also stated in the Senate that you had fixed on October 28 for the slaughter of the optimate party, at a time when many leading citizens fled from Rome not so much to save themselves as to frustrate your plans. You can't deny, can you, that on that very day, hedged in as you were by my guards and watchfulness, you were unable to lift a finger against the state, even as you were proclaiming that you were satisfied, notwithstanding the departure of the rest, with the slaughter of us who had remained?

8. What more? Although you felt sure of taking Praeneste the very first day of November by a night attack, didn't you discover that at my command that colony had been fortified with my garrisons, sentinels, and night watchmen? You make no move, you undertake nothing, you haven't even a single thought that I do not hear of and even see and clearly discern.

Consider finally with me that night before last; then you will realize that I am much more on the alert for the safety of the state than you for its destruction. I say then that on the night before last you came into the quarter of the sickle-makers: I'll be very definite—to the house of Marcus Laeca; and further, that many associates of your criminal madness convened at the same spot. Dare you deny it? Why are you silent? If you object, I will prove your guilt. For I observe that there are present here in the Senate some of those who were together with you.

9. O ye immortal gods! Where in the world are we? What sort of state is ours? In what city do we live? There are here, gentlemen of the Senate, right here in our midst, in the world's most revered and most important legislative body, men who are actually meditating the slaughter of us all and the ruin of this city—nay, of the whole world. I, the consul, see these men before me; I ask for their vote on matters of state; and as yet I do not so much as wound with a word those who ought to be run through with the sword.

You were, therefore, at Laeca's house that night, Catiline; you parceled out the various sections of Italy; you decreed whither you wished each one to set out; you selected those whom you would leave at Rome and those whom you intended to lead out with you; you mapped out portions of the city to be burned; you confirmed (the report) that you would yourself leave in a short time, (although) you said that some little delay was occasioned by the fact that I was yet alive. Two Roman knights were found who should free you of that worry; they promised that on that very night, a little while before daylight, they would assassinate me in my bed.

10. All this I learned when your assembly had scarcely broken up. I made my house secure and fortified it with yet stronger guards. I shut out those whom you had sent in the morning to pay me a formal call, since those very men had made their appearance whose arrival at that time I had previously foretold to many distinguished men. Since this is so, Catiline, proceed with what you have begun. Leave the city at last. The gates are open—go forth! All too long has your Manlian camp been waiting for its commander. Lead out with you too all your henchmen; but if not all, as many as possible. Cleanse the city. You will have delivered me from a great fear if only there is a wall between us. You can dwell amongst us no longer: I will not bear it, I will not suffer it, I will not allow it.

11. Great thanks should be given to the immortal gods, and especially to Jupiter the Stayer, the ancient protector of our city, because we have already so frequently escaped so foul, so horrible, so dangerous a blight on the nation.

The highest interests of the state must not be risked too often in the person of one man. As long as you plotted against me when I was merely consul-elect, Catiline, I protected myself by my personal watchfulness and not by a public guard. When at the last consular elections you tried to kill me, the consul, and your rivals at the voting place, I checked your wicked attempt with the aid and resources of my friends, without arousing any public disturbance. In a word, as often as you sought my life I resisted you on my own initiative, although I realized that my destruction was closely linked with the greatest disaster to the state.

12. But now at last you are openly aiming at the (existence of) the entire nation. The very temples of the immortal gods, the buildings in the city, the life of us all, the whole of Italy you summon to waste and ruin. Therefore, since I dare not yet do what ought above all (to be done), and which is consonant with the sovereign dignity of this people and the precepts of our ancestors, I shall at least do a thing which, if it is too indulgent as regards (due) sternness, is at least very useful for the common safety. For if I order you to be put to death, the rest of your band of conspirators will still remain in the state; but if you leave, as I have so long been urging you to do, your companions will be drained out of the city like so much infested bilge water.

13. What further (can you be waiting for), O Catiline? Can it be that you hesitate to do at my command what you had long been planning to do of your own free will? The consul orders a public enemy to leave the city. "Certainly you don't expect me to go into exile, do you?" you ask. No, I do not command it; but if you ask my advice, I strongly urge (such a course). For is there now anything in this city, Catiline, that can possibly give you pleasure—a city in which there is no one, apart from your own gang of abandoned conspirators, who does not fear you, none who does not hate you? Is there any mark of domestic infamy which has not been branded on your life? Is there any disgrace in personal affairs that does not cling to your reputation? What lust was ever absent from your eyes, what crime from your hands, what shamelessness from your whole body? Is there any young lad, (already) ensnared by your allurements and enticements, to whom you did not offer a sword for his crimes or a torch for his passions?

14. What more? When recently by the death of your first wife you had opened up your home for a new marriage, did you not surpass that first deed with another even more unbelievable crime—a crime which I pass over and gladly allow to remain unmentioned, lest it should seem that in this state so monstrous a crime was ever committed, or that it was left unpunished? I pass over also the downfall of your private fortune, for you will feel the full extent of this calamity on the coming thirteenth of November.

And now I come to matters which are concerned, not with the shame of your personal crimes nor your family troubles and disgrace, but with the highest matters of state and the lives and safety of all of us.

15. How can the sunlight or the air of these heavens be pleasing to you, Catiline, when you realize that not one of these (men) is ignorant of the fact that on December 31, during the consulship of Lepidus and Tullus, you stood in the place of assembly with a weapon? That you had moreover prepared (your) gang for the killing of the consuls and the leading men of the state? That your madness was frustrated not by any fear or reflection on your part, but by the good fortune of the Roman people? But I pass over for the present those (former) deeds— for they are neither unknown nor few which you committed afterward. (But) how often have you (not) attempted to murder me, both while I was consul-elect and even as consul? How many of your thrusts, so

aimed that they seemed impossible to avoid, have I (not) escaped by
a mere twist of the body, as they say. You do nothing, you accomplish
nothing, and yet you give up neither the attempt nor the intention.

16. How often already has the dagger been wrested from your very
hands! How often has it slipped accidentally (from your grasp) and
fallen (to the ground)? Indeed, I must suppose that you have dedicated
and consecrated this dagger to some strange sacred rite, since you
think that it must be planted in the body of the consul. But come now:
what sort of life is this (life) of yours? For I intend now so to speak
to you that I may seem to be actuated, not by righteous hatred, but by
a pity which is in no way your due.

A short while ago you entered the Senate chamber. Was there in
this crowded assembly, among so many of your friends and connections,
a single man who greeted you? If this never happened to another man
within human memory, can you be waiting for any spoken reproach
when you have been condemned by the most weighty verdict of silence?
What (of the fact) that upon your arrival the benches (round about
you) were emptied; that as soon as you sat down all the senators—men
whom you had so often marked out for assassination—left your section
of the seats empty and vacant? In what spirit, think you, should you
encounter (such a rebuff)?

17. By Hercules! If my slaves feared me the way all your fellow
citizens fear you, I should think that I must leave my house. Don't
you then judge it your duty (to leave) the city? Or if I saw that I
was an object of such grave suspicion to my fellow citizens, (even
though) unjustly, and that I was annoying to them, I should prefer
to be deprived of the sight of my countrymen than to be the target
of their angry glances. And you, who from the consciousness of your
crimes know the righteous hatred of all men that has so long been your
due, do you hesitate to shun the sight and the presence of men whose
principles and sensibilities you are outraging? If your own parents
feared and hated you and you were in no way able to appease them,
you would I am sure retire some place out of their sight. But now (it
is) your native land, the universal parent of us all, (that) hates and
fears you, and has long been of the opinion that you are concerned
only with its own impious destruction. Will you not reverence the
authority of this parent, nor bow to its verdict, nor tremble before its
might?

18. Our fatherland, Catiline, deals with you in the following way,
and makes as it were this silent plea: "For some years now no crime

has been committed except by your agency, and no piece of evil-doing has occurred without you. You alone have been permitted to engage with impunity in the slaughtering of countless citizens and in the harassing and plundering of my allies. You have been powerful enough not only to disregard but even to overturn and violate the laws and the law courts. Your earlier crimes were indeed scarcely to be tolerated, yet I bore with them as well as I could. But that now I am utterly terrified on your sole account; that at every rumor Catiline must be feared; that no plot may be concocted against me without some trace of your viciousness—(these continued outrages) I can no longer stomach. Depart, then, and free me from this fear, lest I be overwhelmed if my fear is well-grounded; that at long last I may cease to dread if my fear be not true."

19. If our fatherland were to speak to you in this way, ought it not of right to obtain its request even if it were unable to employ force? What (of the fact) that you (tried to) put yourself into custody, when to rid yourself of suspicion you claimed that you wanted to live at the house of Manius Lepidus? And when he refused to receive you, you had the boldness to come even to me and to ask me to keep you at my house. After I too had replied that I could in no wise live safely in the same house with you, since I should be in grave danger by the very fact that we were hemmed in by the same walls, you betook yourself to the praetor, Quintus Metellus. Finally, rejected in turn by him, you at length made your way to Marcus Metellus, your virtuous crony, who you doubtless imagined would be very solicitous in keeping tab on you, very shrewd in suspecting (your villainies), very resolute in punishing (them)! But how free of the dungeon's chains does it seem that man ought to be who has already adjudged himself worthy of custody?

20. In the light of all this, Catiline, if you cannot resign yourself to death, do you hesitate to depart to some (distant) land, there to give over your life—a life snatched from the many just punishments due to it—to flight and solitude? "Put (this matter of my exile) before the Senate," you say. You make this demand, claiming that if the Senate manifests a desire for your exile, you will bow (to its behest). I will not put (it) before (the Senate)—a step repugnant to my own character; yet I shall enable you to understand what an opinion these (senators) have of you. Leave the city, Catiline; free the state from fear; go into exile, if it is that word you are waiting (to hear). How now? Do you heed anything at all, do you deign to pay any attention to the silence of these (your fellow senators)? They allow it, they are silent. What need to await their spoken command, when you so clearly comprehend the import of their silence?

21. Yet had I addressed this same (command) to Publius Sestius, the fine young man here beside me, or to the courageous Marcus Marcellus, the Senate would ere now have laid violent hands on me, the consul, in this very temple and that with all justice. But with regard to you, Catiline, their very quiet implies approbation; their forbearance is a decree; their silence is itself a ringing shout (of condemnation). Nor (do) only the senators here, whose authority you forsooth hold so dear—and their lives so cheap—(so feel), but also those good and honorable Roman knights and the other brave citizens who are standing around this Senate (building). You had an opportunity to mark their numbers, and to grasp their deep interest (in these proceedings); a short while ago you might even have caught the sound of their shouting. Although I have for some time scarce been able to protect you from their violent hands, yet I shall easily persuade these same citizens to escort you even to the gates (of the city) if only you will turn your back on what you have so long been eager to destroy.

22. And yet why do I keep on talking? (Could it possibly be in the hope) that anything will crush you? That you will ever improve? That you will contemplate flight or seriously consider exile? O that the immortal gods might indeed endow you with such a purpose! And yet, should you take fright at my words and make up your mind to go into exile, I foresee what a storm of hatred will threaten me—if not immediately, on account of the pressing remembrance of your crimes, then certainly in the future. But (the effect) is cheap even at this price, so long as only my personal ruin is involved and the dangers of the state are not involved. Certainly it is too much to ask you to abandon your life of crime, to dread the penalty of law, to give up (your ambitions) at this moment of national crisis. For, Catiline, you are scarcely the type of man whom a sense of decency would ever recall from dishonor, or fear from danger, or good sense from (criminal) madness.

23. Therefore—I say it yet again—away from here! And if, according to your oft-repeated statement, you really wish to fan the flames of hatred against me, your enemy, take the shortest road to exile. If you seize on this expedient, I shall hardly (be able to) put up with the common gossip; if you go into exile at the consul's command, I will scarcely override the wave of unpopularity consequent on your act. But if you would rather do a service to my good name and reputation, set out with your gang of savage criminals, betake yourself to Manlius, stir up (all) abandoned citizens, cut yourself off from (all) decent men, inflict war upon your fatherland, revel in godless brigandage, so that it may be clearly seen that you did not go forth among strangers as (one) cast out by me, but to your own hirelings at my invitation.

24. And yet why should I (speak of) "inviting" you, when I already know that you have sent men ahead to wait for you under arms at Forum Aurelium; when I know that the very day (for the enterprise) has been agreed upon and compacted between yourself and Manlius; when finally your notorious silver eagle, which had its own sacrilegious shrine consecrated at your house—and may it prove a bird of ill-omen to you and yours!—even the eagle has, as I know, been sent ahead? Am I to suppose that you can bear to be separated any longer from that (deity) to which you were wont to pray when setting out on your assassin's work, (and) from whose altar you often betook yourself to the murder of your fellow citizens?

25. You will go at last whither your raging and unbridled passion has so long been hurrying you; and this fact does not cause you any sorrow, but is even the source of some unimaginable pleasure. For this folly did nature itself bring you forth; for this has your will trained you, and fortune preserved you. At all times you have refused, not peace alone, but even war that did not bear the stigma of baseness. You have surrounded yourself with a gang of reprobates gathered from the outcasts (of society), from men who have lost not only fortune but even hope.

26. Among such what joy will you (not) taste! In what pleasures will you (not) revel! With what wild passion will you (not) thrill when amongst so many of your associates you will neither see nor hear a single worthy man! You have an opportunity to display that celebrated endurance of yours (in the face) of hunger, cold, and the lack of all necessities, and by these (same hardships) you will soon feel yourself completely exhausted.

27. This much at least I accomplished in keeping you from the consulship, that now, instead of being able to harass the state as consul, you (are compelled) rather to make an attempt against it as an exile; and that the attempt which you have criminally undertaken should be called brigandage rather than war.

At this point, gentlemen of the Senate, in order that I may ward off and avert an almost justifiable complaint of the nation, I beg you to consider most carefully what I am about to say, and to let it sink deep into your minds. For if our fatherland, much dearer to me than life itself, if the whole of Italy and the entire nation should ask me: "Marcus Tullius, what are you about? Do you intend to let go scot-free a man whom you have discovered to be a public enemy, who you know will be the leader of a war, and who you feel is being awaited as general in the camp of the enemy—this instigator of evil, this orig-inator of conspiracy, this inciter of slaves and reprobate citizens? Will you, I say, let him go in such a way that he will seem to have been not so much expelled from the city as rather impelled against it by you? Won't you order this fellow to be dragged to prison, to be hurried off to death, to be executed by capital punishment?

28. "What can it be that holds you back? The practice of our an-cestors? Why, often enough even private citizens of this nation pun-ished dangerous citizens with death. Or can it be the laws that have been passed respecting the punishment of Roman citizens? But in our state national traitors have never enjoyed the rights of citizens. Is it the hatred of future generations that you fear? You would surely be exhibiting a strange gratitude to the Roman people if for fear of un-popularity or danger you were unmindful of the safety of your fellow citizens; for it has in so short a time raised you, a man of undis-tinguished ance. try, recognized merely for your own merit, through all the curule offices to the highest position of authority.

29. "But if there is indeed some fear of unpopularity, then cer-tainly the hatred consequent on austere courage is much to be pre-ferred to that which results from inactivity and criminal negligence. Or don't you suppose that when Italy will be laid waste, her cities harassed and her houses in flames, that then truly you will be seared with the hot breath of hatred?"

To these holy words of my country and of those men who are of like mind, I make the following brief reply: If I believed, gentlemen of the Senate, that the best course of action were to punish Catiline with death, I would not have granted that professional thug a single hour of grace. For if our noblest and most distinguished citizens, far from being polluted by the blood of Saturninus and the Gracchi and Flaccus and many another (victim) of bygone days, were even covered with fresh honor (by their deeds), I should certainly not have to fear that the killing of this civic parricide would result in any future un-popularity to myself. And even though such a result were to threaten me to the greatest possible extent, still my mettle has ever been such that I would hold unpopularity gained by courageous action not as unpopularity, but as a glory.

30. And yet there are some in this Senate who either do not see what is impending or are dissembling what they see. These men have nourished Catiline's hope by their mild sentiments, and by their incredulity have strengthened the nascent conspiracy. Under the influence of such men, too, many others, not evil men only but the merely inexperienced as well, would say that I had acted cruelly and despotically had I proceeded against this criminal. Now I see clearly that if Catiline arrives at Manlius' camp whither he is bound, no one will be so stupid as not to see that a conspiracy has been formed, none so outrageous as to deny it. But I realize too that if Catiline alone is killed, this curse of the state will receive but a momentary check, and cannot be blotted out for good. If on the other hand Catiline leaves the city, taking with him his associates and adding to them all the other castaways whom he has picked up on many shores, then there will be trampled down and utterly destroyed not only this rank weed of rebellion, already grown too tall, but even the very root and seed of all evils.

31. For it is true, gentlemen of the Senate, that we have been involved for some time in the dangerous toils of conspiracy; and yet, somehow or other, the culmination of all crimes and old madness and daring has burst forth as it were against the year of my consulship. If from so numerous a band or brigands Catiline alone is removed, it will perhaps seem for some short time that we have been relieved of our worry and fear; but the poison will really remain behind, penned up within the veins and vital organs of the state. Just as men sick with a serious disease, when they are tossed about in the burning heat of fever seem at first to be relieved if they drink cold water but then are much more severely distressed, so this sickness which is in the state, if temporarily relieved by the punishment of this one man, will only grow very much worse, as long as the rest remain alive.

32. Therefore let these wretches go off by themselves; let them cut themselves off from all decent men; let them gather together into one place; finally, as I have often said before, let a wall separate us from them. Let them stop laying ambushes for the consul at his own house; let them give up surrounding the tribunal of the urban praetor, and besieging the Senate house with their swords, and making ready firebrands and torches for setting the city on fire. Finally, let each and every one of them have stamped on his forehead his opinion of our sovereign state. I promise you, gentlemen of the Senate, that so great

will be the watchfulness of us the consuls, so great your authority, so great the courage of the Roman knights, and so unanimous the agreement of all right-minded citizens, that at the departure of Catiline you will see all (crimes) laid bare and brought to light, checked, and avenged.

33. Under such portents, then, O Catiline, go forth to your godless and wicked war, bringing down upon the state a happy deliverance from peril, but upon yourself a damnable ruin, and destruction upon those satellites of your every crime and murder.

And do thou, Jupiter, thou who wert established by Romulus (as our protector) under the same sacred auguries as Rome itself, and whom we truly call the firm bulwark of this city and its sovereign rule—do thou, I say, ward off this enemy and his associates from your own and other shrines, from the dwellings and walls of Rome, from the life and well-being of all its citizens; and mayest thou visit with never-ending retribution, both in life and after death, men who are the enemies of decent people, the foes of their fatherland, the despoilers of Italy, the associates of a criminal alliance and a shameful league.

THIRD ORATION AGAINST CATILINE

1. Citizens of Rome, you this day behold your commonwealth, the lives of all of you, your property, fortunes, wives, and children, and the seat of this illustrious empire, our happy and beautiful city, snatched from fire and sword and almost from the jaws of doom, and preserved and restored to you, thanks to the extraordinary love of the immortal gods toward you, thanks to my toil, plans, and peril.

2. And if those days on which we are preserved are no less pleasant and memorable to us than those on which we are born, because the joy of safety is a certain one while the circumstances of birth are uncertain, and because we are born without any consciousness but are preserved with pleasure, certainly, since we elevate to the heavens with affection and renown the founder of this city, the savior of this same city after its foundation and extension ought to be held in honor among you and your descendants.

For we have quenched the fires which had been set to and had all but surrounded the entire city, the temples, shrines, houses, and walls, and we also blunted the swords that had been drawn against the commonwealth, and dashed their points from your throats.

3. Since these facts have been brought to light, laid bare, and discovered in the Senate through my efforts, I shall now give a brief explanation of them to you, gentlemen of Rome, so that you who are uninformed and anxious may be able to know the extent and manner of my investigations and discoveries.

To begin with, ever since Catiline a few days ago burst forth from the city, while he had left behind him at Rome the companions of his crime, scheming leaders of this wicked war, I have always been on the watch, making provisions, gentlemen of Rome, whereby we may possibly be saved amid these extremely well-hidden snares.

For at that time when I threw Catiline out—I now indeed no longer fear the unpopularity of this term, since the fact that he got out alive is much more fearful—but at that time when I desired his banishment, I was of the opinion that either the rest of his conspiratorial band would depart at the same time or that those who remained would be weak and powerless without him.

4. As for me, when I saw that those whom I knew to be aflame with extreme rage and crime were with us and had remained at Rome, I spent all my days and nights in the effort to understand and see their actions and schemes, so that, since my words were gaining less confidence in your ears because of the unbelievable extent of the crime, I might so get a grasp of the situation that you might at long last make provisions in your attitude (minds) for your safety, when you beheld the evil deed itself with your own eyes.

And so, when I found that the embassy of the Allobroges had been approached by Publius Lentulus for the purpose of exciting a war across the Alps and an uprising in Gaul, and (when I had learned) that they had been sent into Gaul to their own fellow citizens, that on the same trip (they had been sent) with letters and injunctions, that joined to them as fellow traveler was Titus Volturcius, and that letters had been given to him for Catiline, I thought that an opportunity had been offered me—one difficult (to obtain) but one I had always prayed for from the immortal gods—an opportunity, namely, whereby the entire situation might clearly be grasped not only by me, but also by the Senate and by you.

5. So yesterday I called before me the praetors, Lucius Flaccus and Gaius Pomptinus, brave and patriotic men; I explained the situation; I showed them what I wanted done; and they, because their feelings toward the government were extraordinarily high, undertook the business without any refusal or delay; and as dusk was coming on, secretly came to the Mulvian Bridge, and there so divided themselves into two sections in the estates near by that the bridge and the Tiber were between them.

There also they had led many brave men without any suspicion on the part of anyone; and I had sent many armed young men, selected from the prefecture of Reate, whose assistance I constantly use in the state as a protection.

6. Meanwhile, about three o'clock in the morning, as the embassy of the Allobroges was beginning to cross the Mulvian Bridge with a large retinue and with Volturcius along, an attack is launched against them; swords are drawn by their men and by ours. The situation was known to the praetors only; it was not known to the rest.

Then with the intervention of Pomptinus and Flaccus the fight quieted down. What letters there were in the retinue are handed over to the praetors with seals unbroken; the men themselves are arrested and brought to me at daybreak.

I immediately summoned before me the most wicked contriver of all these crimes, Cimber Gabinius, himself as yet suspecting nothing; next Lucius Statilius was also sent for and after him Gaius Cethegus; last of all came Lentulus—I take it because, contrary to his custom, he had stayed up all the night before writing letters.

7. When the leading men of note of this city, who on hearing of the arrest had come to me in crowds in the morning, were in favor of my opening the letters before they were brought to the Senate, lest, if nothing was found in them, such an extreme confusion appear heedlessly to have been thrust upon the state by me, I said I would not cause the entire matter of a public peril to fail to be brought before the public council.

For, gentlemen of Rome, even if those facts which had been brought to me had not been discovered, yet I did not think I need have feared excessive carefulness in so extraordinary a crisis of the state.

8. I got together a large senatorial gathering, as you have seen; and meanwhile, upon the advice of the Allobroges, I immediately sent Gaius Sulpicius, the praetor, a brave man, to bring from Cethegus' house what weapons were there, if any. From his house he brought a very large number of daggers and swords.

I brought Volturcius in without the Gauls. At the bidding of the Senate I gave him a pledge in the name of the state. I exhorted him fearlessly to indicate what he knew. Then, when he had scarcely recovered himself from his great fear, he said that he had instructions and letters from Publius Lentulus to Catiline (to the effect) that he should use the protection of slaves, that he should come up to the city with his army as soon as possible; with this in view, that, when they had set fire to the city in all directions just as had been mapped out and allotted, and when they had made an extensive slaughter of citizens, he (Catiline) might be at hand to intercept the refugees and join hands with these leaders in the city.

9. When the Gauls had been brought in, they alleged that an oath and letters for their people had been given them by Lentulus, Cethegus, and Statilius, and that they had been ordered by these men and by Lucius Cassius to send their cavalry into Italy as soon as possible; that there would be no lack of infantry; that Lentulus had given them assurance from Sibylline utterances and the answers of the soothsayers that he was that third Cornelius to whom the rule of this city and empire must needs fall; before him there had been Cinna and Sulla; and that he himself had also said that this was the year of doom for the destruction of this city and empire because it was the tenth year after the acquittal of the Vestal virgins and the twentieth after the burning of the capital.

10. But they said that there had been this disagreement between Cethegus and the others, that it pleased Lentulus and the rest that the slaughter and burning of the city should take place on the feast of the Saturnalia, (while) to Cethegus this seemed much too long (a time).

And to make a long story short, gentlemen of Rome, we ordered the letters which were alleged to have been written by each individual to be brought forth. First we showed Cethegus his seal. He recognized it. We cut the thread. We read.

There was written in his own hand to the Senate and people of the Allobroges that he would do those things which he had assured their envoys; that he prayed that they would likewise do what things their envoys received from him.

Then Cethegus, although just a moment before he had yet made some reply about the swords and daggers which had been seized at his house and had alleged that he had always been an ardent collector of fine weapons, when his letter had been read aloud, broken in spirit and downcast because of his consciousness (of guilt), straightway fell silent.

11. Statilius was brought in. He recognized both his seal and his handwriting. Letters were read aloud in pretty much the same tenor. He pleaded guilty.

Then I showed Lentulus his letters, and asked him whether or not he recognized the seal. He nodded assent. " 'Tis indeed," I said, "an extremely well-known seal, the picture of your grandfather, a very famous man, who had a unique love for his country and fellow citizens; a picture indeed which, silent though it was, should have restrained you from so foul a crime."

Letters on the same plan to the Senate and people of the Allobroges are read. I offered him an opportunity to make any statement in the matter if he wished.

And for his part, at first he denied (it all); but after a bit, when the entire charge had been put forth in public, he rose to his feet. He asked the Gauls what business he had with them, why they had come to his house; (he asked) the same of Volturcius. When they had made brief and steadfast reply, saying through whom and how often they had come to him, and had asked him whether he had made no statement to them about the Sibylline utterances, then on a sudden, maddened with crime, he gave proof of the violence of his consciousness (of guilt).

12. For although he could have denied the charge, suddenly, contrary to the opinion of everyone, he pleaded guilty. And so there failed him not only his well-known gift and experience in public speaking, which was always his strong point, but also, because of the violence of the crime which had been clearly detected, (there failed him) both his impudence, in which he outclassed everyone, and his depravity.

But Volturcius immediately orders the letters, which allegedly had been given to him for Catiline, to be brought in and opened. And although violently disturbed at this point, Lentulus none the less recognized both his handwriting and his seal. It was anonymous, but ran thus:

"You will learn my identity from him whom I have sent to you. Have a care that you play the man, and consider how far you have gone. See what your needs are, and look to it that you join to you the forces of everybody, even of the most lowly."

Next when Gabinius had been brought in, although at first he began to answer arrogantly, he ended by denying none of the alleged charges of the Gauls.

13. As for me, gentlemen of Rome, although the letters, seals, handwriting, and last of all the individual confessions appeared most sure arguments and evidences of crime, still more certain (evidence) seemed these things—their color, their eyes, their expression, and their silence.

For they were so dumfounded, they so gazed at the ground, they occasionally so exchanged furtive glances, that they seemed not to be indicted by others but to be indicting themselves.

When the charges had been brought up and made, gentlemen of Rome, I consulted the Senate on what action it desired taken in this grave public matter. Some very harsh and uncompromising proposals were introduced by leading members, and these the Senate passed without any amendments. And since the bill has not yet been entirely written up, I will explain to you from memory the decision of the Senate.

First of all a vote of thanks is extended to me in unstinting terms, because the state has been freed from extreme perils thanks to my manliness, my strategy, my foresight. Next, Lucius Flaccus and Gaius Pomptinus, the praetors, get a justly deserved share of praise because I used their brave and faithful services. And even upon my stout-hearted colleague in the consulship some praise is bestowed because he had kept those who took part in this conspiracy far removed from his own aims and those of the state.

14. And so the Senate voted in favor of holding Publius Lentulus in custody after his resignation of the praetorship; likewise (they declared) that Gaius Cethegus, Lucius Statilius, and Publius Gabinius, all of whom were present, should be given into custody; and the very same sentence was passed on Lucius Cassius, who had claimed for himself the charge of setting fire to the city; (the same) against Marcus Ceparius, to whom, it was pointed out, Apulia had been designated for the stirring up of the shepherds; (the same) against Publius Furius, who comes from those settlers whom Lucius Sulla had sent to Faesule; (the same) against Quintus Annius Chilo, who had always dealt with Furius in the matter of inciting the Allobroges; (the same) against Publius Umbrenus, a freedman, by whom it was evident the Gauls were first taken to Gabinius.

Furthermore, the Senate used such leniency, gentlemen of Rome, that by the punishment of the nine most wicked members of this extensive plot and of this great crowd of civil enemies it was thought that the attitude of the rest could be healed, in view of the fact that the state had been preserved.

15. And also a public act of thanksgiving to the immortal gods for their unique favor has been decreed in my name because I was the first since the foundation of the city to whose lot it fell as a civil magistrate—to quote from the decree—"to free the city from fire, the citizens from slaughter, and Italy from war." And if we set up a comparison between this thanksgiving and other public acts of thanksgiving, there is this difference, that the others were voted because of the successful administration of the commonwealth, this one alone for its salvation.

And that which had to be done first, has been done and is over with. For Publius Lentulus, although in view of the clarification of the charges and his own admissions he had in the opinion of the Senate lost his right not only to the praetorship but even to citizenship; none the less resigned his office, so that we are spared that scruple in the punishment of Publius Lentulus as a private citizen which did not prevent the illustrious Gaius Marius from executing Gaius Glaucius, a praetor, against whom as an individual no decree had been passed.

16. Now, gentlemen of Rome, because you hold the wicked ringleaders of a criminally dangerous war in captivity and under arrest, you ought to regard all the forces of Catiline, all his hopes and resources, as having fallen, now that these dangers to our city have been banished.

When indeed I was driving him (Catiline) from the city, I had this in mind, gentlemen of Rome, that with the removal of Catiline I need not have feared Publius Lentulus' drowsiness, nor Lucius Cassius' corpulence, nor the hot-headed heedlessness of Gaius Cethegus.

He, and he only, had to be feared from that whole group, but that only so long as he was (kept) within the city walls. He knew everything; he had the approach to everyone; he had the power and the nerve to call upon, to sound out, and to tempt. He had a genius suited to crime, yet did his genius lack neither action (hand) nor words (tongue). He had definite men chosen and assigned to the execution of definite jobs. Nor indeed, when he had given any order did he take it for granted that it had been executed, there was nothing he himself would not undergo, encounter, look out for, and toil for; he could stand cold, thirst, and hunger.

17. Unless I had driven this man (who was) so sharp, so brazen, so prepared, so crafty, so wide-awake in crime, and so painstaking in shameful deeds from secret internal plots into open brigandage—I shall speak my mind, gentlemen of Rome—I would not easily have lifted this ponderous weight of evil from your necks.

He would not have determined upon the Saturnalia for us, nor would he have threatened the day of destruction and doom for the commonweal so long beforehand, nor would he have allowed his seal, his letters—clear witness of crime—to be seized.

Now, in his absence, all this has so been executed that no petty theft in a private house has ever been discovered as much in the open as this extensive plot against the state has been clearly found out and arrested.

But if Catiline had remained in town to this day—although as long as he did, I met and blocked his every scheme—yet, to say the least, we would have had to fight it out with him, nor would we ever, as long as he was in town as an enemy, have freed the state from these extreme perils so peacefully, so tranquilly, and so silently.

And yet this entire business, gentlemen of Rome, has been conducted by me in such a way as to seem to have been done and provided for by the will and design of the immortal gods.

21. For who can be so hostile to truth, gentlemen of Rome, so hasty, and so foolish as to deny that everything we see, and especially this city, is governed by the will and power of the immortal gods?

Indeed, when an (oracular) answer had been given, (saying) that slaughter, fire, and the destruction of the commonwealth were being made ready, and this at the hands of citizens, (a prophecy) which at the time because of the vastness of the crimes appeared unbelievable to not a few, you realize that those crimes have not only been devised in the minds of wicked citizens, but have even been undertaken.

Is not the following incident *(illud)* so much (a token) of divine assistance *(praesens)* as to seem to have been done by Jupiter Optimus Maximus—(the fact, namely) that when this very day both the conspirators and their accusers were this morning being brought through the forum to the Temple of Concord at my command, at that very moment the statue was being erected?

And when it had been set up facing you and the Senate, you saw everything which had been devised against the safety of all brought to light and laid bare.

22. Those shameful men are the more deserving of hatred and punishment because they made an attempt to set their death dealing and wicked fires not only to your homes and houses, but even in the temples of the gods and their shrines.

And if I should say I was the one who blocked them, I would take too much credit upon myself and would be intolerable; he it was—he, Jupiter, it was—who blocked them, he it was who desired the preservation of the Capitoline Hill, of these temples, of the entire city, and of all of you. It was under the leadership of the immortal gods that I took on this attitude of mind and determination of will and arrived at these amazing indictments.

For indeed matters of such importance would surely never so madly have been entrusted by Lentulus and the other enemies of the state to unknown foreigners unless reason had been snatched away by the immortal gods from such a reckless enterprise.

What else? That men of Gaul, from a state but imperfectly pacified, which is the only nation remaining that seems able and not unwilling to declare war against the Roman people, (that such men) should disregard their hope for empire and their hope for the greatest advantages, offered them unsolicited by members of the aristocracy, and that they should prefer your safety before their own wealth—do you not regard that as having been accomplished by divine intervention, especially so since they could have conquered us not by fighting but by keeping silent?

23. Therefore, gentlemen of Rome, since a public thanksgiving has been decreed at all the shrines, celebrate those days with your wives and children. Indeed many honors have always rightly and justly been accorded the immortal gods—but never before more justly, for you have been snatched from a cruel and wretched disaster, you have been snatched away without slaughter, without bloodshed, without an army, and without a struggle. In the garb of peace, with me, your leader and commander, in the garb of peace, have you won the day.

24. For call to mind, gentlemen of Rome, all the civil strifes, not only those about which you have heard, but also those which you yourselves remember to have seen. Lucius Sulla checked Publius Sulpicius; as for Gaius Marius, the guardian of this city, and many other brave men, some he banished from the state, others he killed. Gnaeus Octavius the consul drove his colleague from the city at the point of the sword; all this section here overflowed with heaps of corpses and the blood of citizens.

Cinna gained control afterwards together with Marius; then indeed, with the murder of outstanding men, the lights of the state were snuffed out. Next Sulla avenged the savagery of this victory—there is no need even to mention with what wholesale loss of citizens and how great disaster to the state.

Marcus Lepidus had a falling out with the distinguished and fearless Quintus Catulus; the downfall of the former brought not nearly so much grief to the state as that of others.

25. And yet all those struggles were of such a kind as not to have any relation to the destruction of the commonwealth but to its reformation. Those men did not desire that there should be no commonwealth, but that they should be the leaders in the commonwealth as it existed; nor did they desire to burn this city, but to flourish in it.

Further, all those struggles, none of which sought the destruction of the commonwealth, were of such a nature as to have been settled not by the restoration of peace, but by the massacre of citizens.

In this savage war, unique in the history of mankind—a war such as no barbarian people has ever waged with its own people, a war in which the law set down by Lentulus, Catiline, Cethegus, and Cassius was this, that everyone who after the preservation of the city could be rescued should be led away in the number of the enemy—I so conducted myself, gentlemen of Rome, as to keep you all in safety; and when your enemies had thought that the number of citizens surviving should be in proportion to the number who had outlived an endless massacre and that only so much of the city should remain as could not be touched by fire, I preserved both the city and the citizens safe and sound.

26. For all these benefits, gentlemen of Rome, I demand of you no reward for valor, no mark of honor, no memorial of praise other than the everlasting memory of this day. In your hearts (memories) do I desire all my triumphs, all my decorations of honor, all my memorials of glory, and all my marks of praise to find their foundation and erection.

Nothing mute can delight me, nothing silent, nothing, finally, of the sort which the less worthy are able to attain. In your memory, gentlemen of Rome, will our achievements be nourished, in your talk will they increase, in the monuments of your literature will they grow to maturity and strength; and I understand that the same period of history *(diem)*, which I hope will be everlasting, has been granted both for the salvation of the city and the memory of my term in the office of consul, and that at one and the same period there have existed in this commonwealth two citizens of whom one put boundaries not of land but of the heavens upon the territory of your empire, the other preserved the seat and capital of this same empire.

27. But because the outcome and circumstances of the deeds I have done are not the same as those of men who have waged foreign wars, because I have now to live with men whom I have overcome and crushed, whereas they have left their enemy behind either destroyed or in subjugation, it is your responsibility, gentlemen of Rome, to see to it that if their deeds proved an advantage to others, my deeds may not at any time prove harmful to me. For I have seen to it that the

wicked and criminal schemes of brazen men could do you no harm; it is yours to see to it that they do me no harm.

And yet, gentlemen of Rome, I myself indeed can suffer no harm at the hands of those men. For there is a great protection in good men—a protection which has been stored up for me for all time. There is a great sense of honor in the state, which will ever be my silent defendant. There is a great strength in a sense (of guilt), and those who disregard it will give themselves away when they wish to harm me.

28. For I am of such mind, gentlemen of Rome, as not only to yield to the daring of no one, but also as without provocation to challenge all criminals.

And if the entire attack of civil enemies, now that it has been beaten off from you, turns against me alone, it will be yours to see to it, gentlemen of Rome, how you wish those men hereafter to fare who expose themselves to hatred and all sorts of dangers for your safety; as for me myself, what is there that can be added to the fruits of my life, especially since I see no higher steps either in your honor or the glory of virtue to which I may desire to climb.

29. This much I certainly shall do, gentlemen of Rome, namely, guard and enhance in my private life the deeds I have done in my consulship, so that if any hatred in the preservation of the commonwealth has been incurred, it may injure those who hate, but turn to my glory. Finally, I shall so conduct myself in the state as always to be mindful of my past deeds and careful to make it appear that they were done by strength of character, not by luck.

As for you, gentlemen of Rome, now that it is night pay worship to the great Jupiter, guardian of this city and your guardian. Depart to your houses; and although the danger has been dispelled, yet defend them just as much as the night before last with sentinels and guards. That you may no longer be forced to do so and that you may be able to live in lasting peace shall be my care.

THE IMPEACHMENT OF GAIUS VERRES[1]

"**1.** Gentlemen of the Court: At this great political crisis, there seems to have been offered to you, not through man's wisdom but almost as the direct gift of heaven, the very thing that was most to be

---

[1] This section is from *Cicero: The Verrine Orations,* translated by L. H. G. Greenwood. Reprinted from the Loeb Classical Library by permission of the President and Fellows of Harvard College.

desired; a thing that will help, more than anything else, to mitigate the unpopularity of your Order and the discredit attaching to these Courts of Law. A belief has by this time established itself, as harmful to the whole nation as it is perilous to yourselves, and everywhere expressed not merely by our own people but by foreigners as well: the belief that these Courts, constituted as they now are, will never convict any man, however guilty, if only he has money.

"2. And now, at the moment of supreme danger for your Order and your judicial privileges, when preparations have been made for an attempt, by means of public meetings and proposals for legislation, to fan the flames of senatorial unpopularity, Gaius Verres appears, to stand his trial before you: a man already condemned, in the world's opinion, by his life and deeds; already acquitted, according to his own confident assertions, by his vast fortune. . . .

"May I make you a personal confession, gentlemen? Many are the stealthy attacks that Verres has delivered against me by land and sea, some of which I have eluded by my own carefulness, repelling the rest with the help of my energetic and loyal friends. Yet never have I felt myself facing such grave danger, nor been so thoroughly alarmed, as now when the trial has begun.

"4. And it is not the eagerness with which my speech for the prosecution is awaited, nor the huge crowd assembled here, that thus affects me, profoundly disturbing as these things are to me: it is rather the unscrupulous assault that Verres is secretly attempting to launch, at once against myself, and you, and the praetor Manius Glabrio, and the Roman nation, and their allies, and the foreign world, and the senatorial order, and all that the Senate means and is. He goes about saying that people have reason to fear the consequences of filching enough for themselves only, but that he himself has carried off enough for a great many people; that no sanctuary is too holy for money to defile it, no fortress too strong for money to capture it. . . .

"7. Let me tell you of the impudent and insane plan that is now in his mind. It is plain to him that I am approaching this case so well equipped and prepared for it that I shall be able to pin him down as a robber and a criminal, not merely in the hearing of this Court, but before the eyes of the whole world. He sees how many senators, and how many Roman knights, have come to testify to his evil violence; he sees also the throng of those, citizens of our own and of allied states, to whom he has himself done conspicuous wrong; he sees, too, from communities that are among our best friends, how many deputations, formed of responsible men and armed with official documents, are assembled here against him.

"8. But in spite of this, he holds so low an opinion of the whole upper class, he believes the senatorial Courts to be so utterly abandoned and corrupt, that he goes about remarking openly what good reason he had to set his heart on making money, since he finds his money such a tower of strength to him; how he bought himself the hardest thing to buy, the right date for his own trial, so that he might be able to buy all else the more easily afterwards, and since he could not possibly escape the rough waters of prosecution, might at least avoid the gales of the stormy season.

"9. And yet if he could have placed any trust, I do not say in the strength of his case, but in any honourable kind of defence, in the eloquence, or in the popularity, of any of his supporters, he would certainly not have been driving and hunting such game as that; he would not have held a view of the senatorial order so low and contemptuous as to set about the selection of a senator, chosen by his own caprice, to be the object of a prosecution, and to stand his trial first, while he himself meanwhile was making the preparations he needed.

"10. Now, in all this, I can see easily enough what his hopes are, and what ends he has in view: but with such a court and such a president of the court as we now have sitting here, I do fail to understand how he can expect to gain his ends at all. One thing alone I do understand—and the people of Rome were convinced of this when the challenging of the judges took place: his hopes were of such a kind that he looked upon his money as his only possible means of escape, and never supposed that, if this support were taken from him, anything else could help him.

"And indeed what brain could be powerful enough, what eloquence ready or rich enough, to defend with even partial success the career of Verres, a career convicted already of countless vices and countless crimes, and condemned long ago by the feelings, and by the judgement, of all the world? . . .

"But nowhere did he multiply and magnify the memorials and the proofs of all his evil qualities so thoroughly as in his governorship of Sicily; which island for the space of three years he devastated and ruined so effectually that nothing can restore it to its former condition, and it hardly seems possible that a long lapse of years and a succession of upright governors can in time bring it a partial revival of prosperity.

"13. So long as Verres was governing it, its people were protected neither by their own laws, nor by the decrees of the Roman Senate, nor by the rights that belong to all nations alike. None of them has anything left today, except what either escaped the notice of this avaricious and intemperate ruffian, or remained over when his greed was glutted. . . .

"15. Is it alleged that he did these things so secretly that they were not known everywhere? I do not believe that one human being lives, who has heard the name of Verres spoken, and cannot also repeat the tale of his evil doings. I have therefore more reason to fear criticism for passing over charges of which he is guilty, than for inventing against him charges of which he is innocent. And indeed the purpose of the great audience that has gathered to attend this trial is not, I conceive, to learn the facts of the case from me, but to join me in reviewing the facts that it knows already.

"The knowledge of all these things has led this abandoned madman to adopt a new method of fighting me. It is not his real purpose to find an eloquent advocate to oppose me. He relies upon no man's popularity or influence or power. He does indeed pretend that it is here his confidence lies; but I can see what his purpose is, of which, to be sure, he makes no great secret. He displays against me a hollow show of titled names, the names of a very arrogant set of persons, who harm my cause by their being noble less than they forward it by their being known: and he pretends to put his trust in their protection, while all the time he has been engineering a quite different scheme.

"16. I will explain briefly to you, gentlemen, the hope that now possesses him, and the object of his present exertions: but before coming to that, I will ask you to note what he was aiming at in the earlier stages of this affair.

"No sooner was he back from his province than he bought up this Court for a large sum of money. The terms of the contract held good as arranged, until the challenging took place. When the challenging had taken place—since the good destiny of our country had prevailed over Verres' hopes when the lots were cast, and when the members of the Court were challenged my carefulness prevailed over the effrontery of him and his supporters—the contractor threw up his undertaking entirely. Everything now promised well.

"17. The list of your names, as members of this Court, was accessible to everyone: this verdict, it seemed, could be given without any fear that special signs, colours, or smudges could be marked upon the voting-tablets. Verres from looking lively and cheerful, had been plunged suddenly into so gloomy a state of depression, that he was looked on as an already condemned man by everyone in Rome, himself included.

"And now behold, equally suddenly, within these last few days, since the result of the consular elections has been known, the same old methods are being set going again, and more money than before is being spent upon them: the same insidious attacks are being organized, by the same agents, upon your good name, gentlemen, and upon the well-being of the community at large. This fact was first revealed to me by a slender thread of circumstantial evidence; but once the door was opened to admit suspicion, a direct path led me to the inmost secrets of Verres and his friends. . . .

"**20.** For they argued thus, and honest gentlemen kept saying so to one another and to me, that it was at last unmistakably plain that our law-courts were worthless. An accused man one day regards his own condemnation as an accomplished fact, and the next day is acquitted by the election of his advocate to the consulship?

"Why, is the presence at Rome of all Sicily and its inhabitants, of all its business men, of all its public and private records—is all this, then, to count for nothing? No, not if the consul-elect will not have it so. Why, will the Court have no regard for the statements of the prosecution, the evidence of the witnesses, the credit of the Roman nation? No; everything is to be steered and directed by the hand of one powerful man.

"I will speak frankly, gentlemen. This circumstance disturbed me profoundly. Everywhere the soundest men were saying, 'Verres will certainly escape your clutches, but the law-courts will be in our keeping no longer; for who can possibly hesitate about transferring them to other hands, if Verres is acquitted?'

"**21.** Everyone was distressed; less disturbed, however, by this scoundrel's sudden exultation, than by this unheard-of speech of congratulation from a man of such high position. I did my best to pretend that I felt no uneasiness myself; I did my best, with the help of calm looks and silence, to mask and conceal the anguish that I felt.

"But to my surprise, only a few days later, when the praetors-elect were casting lots, and it fell to Marcus Metellus to be president of the Extortion Court, I received the news that Verres had been so warmly congratulated on this that he even sent off slaves to his house to carry the news to his wife.

"**22.** Now I admit that the way the lot had fallen was a new source of regret to me: but still, I could not see what special reason I had to be alarmed by it. One thing I did learn from certain persons who were my regular detectives: that a number of baskets of Sicilian money had been transferred from a particular senator to a particular knight, that some ten or more of these baskets were left at this senator's house for a purpose connected with my own candidature, and that a meeting of the bribery-agents for all the tribes was held one night at Verres' house.

"23. One of these agents, a man who felt bound to give me all the help he could, called on me that same night, and told me what Verres had been saying to them: he had reminded them how liberally he had dealt with them, both when he was himself a candidate for the praetorship some time ago, and at the recent elections of consuls and praetors; and then had at once proceeded to promise them what they chose to ask for turning me out of my aedileship. At this, some of them had said they would not dare to try it, others had replied that they did not believe it could be managed; however, a stout ally turned up from among his own kinsmen, Quintus Verres of the Romilian tribe, a fine old specimen of the bribery-agent, who had been the pupil and friend of Verres' father; this man undertook to manage the business for £5,000 down, and some of the others said after all that they would join him. In view of all this my friend very kindly warned me to take every possible precaution. . . .

"27. Indeed? did you count on my saying nothing of so serious a matter? on my caring for anything, when the country and my own reputation are in such danger, except my duty and my honour? The second consul-elect sent for the Sicilians, and some of them came, remembering that Lucius Metellus was now praetor in Sicily. He talked to them in this sort of way: 'I am consul; one of my brothers is governing Sicily, the other is going to preside over the Extortion Court; many steps have been taken to secure that no harm can happen to Verres.'

"28. To attempt to intimidate witnesses, especially these timorous and calamity-stricken Sicilians, not merely by your personal influence, but by appealing to their awe of you as consul, and to the power of the two praetors—if this is not judicial corruption, Metellus, I should be glad to know what is. What would you not do for an innocent kinsman, if you forsake duty and honour for an utter rascal who is no kin of yours at all, and make it possible for those who do not know you to believe in the truth of his allegations concerning you? . . .

"**32.** And now, gentlemen, I should really like to ask you what, in your opinion, I ought to do: for I am sure the unspoken advice that you give me will be to do just that which my own understanding shows me I am bound to do. If I spend upon my speech the full time allotted me by law, I shall indeed secure some return to myself for all my toilsome and concentrated exertions; my conduct of this prosecution will show that no man in all history ever came into court more ready and watchful and well-prepared than I come now. But there is the gravest danger that, while I am thus reaping the credit due to my hard work, the man I am prosecuting will slip through my fingers. What, then, can be done? A thing that is surely plain and obvious enough.

"**33.** The harvest of fame that might have been gathered by making a long continuous speech let us reserve for another occasion, and let us now prosecute our man by means of documents and witnesses, the written statements and official pronouncements of private persons and public bodies. It is you, Hortensius, with whom I shall have to reckon throughout. I will speak frankly. If I could suppose that, in this case, your method of opposing me was that of fair speech in palliation of the charges I am bringing, I too would be for devoting my energies to a speech for the prosecution setting forth the charges in full. But since, as it is, you have chosen to fight me in a way less well suited to your own personal character than to the emergency in which Verres finds himself and to the badness of Verres' case, tactics such as you have adopted must somehow or other be countered.

"**34.** Your plan is, that you should not begin your speech for the defence till both the festivals are over. My plan is, to reach the adjournment of the case before the first festival begins. It amounts to this, that you will have the credit of planning an ingenious move, and I of making the inevitable reply to it.

"But with regard to what I began just now to speak of—that it is you with whom I have to reckon—what I mean is this. Although, when I undertook this case at the request of the Sicilians, I felt that there was a full measure of honour for me in the fact that the people who had made trial of my integrity and self-control were willing now to make trial of my good faith and energy: yet the task once undertaken, I put before myself a still greater object, whereby to let the Roman people perceive my loyalty to my country.

"**35.** For I reflected that to prosecute in court a man who already stood condemned by the court of humanity was a task very far from worthy of the toil and effort it would cost me, were it not that your intolerably despotic power, and the self-seeking that you have exhibited in more than one trial of recent years, were being engaged once more in the defence of that desperate scoundrel yonder. But as things now stand, since you take so much pleasure in all this tyrannical domination of our courts of law, and since men do exist who find nothing shameful, nothing disgusting, in their own wanton deeds and vile reputations, but appear to challenge, as though of set purpose, the hatred and anger of the people of Rome: I will declare boldly, that the burden I have shouldered may indeed be heavy and dangerous for myself, but is nevertheless such that my manhood and determination may fitly strain every muscle to bear it.

"36. Since the whole of our poorer class is being oppressed by the hand of recklessness and crime, and groaning under the infamy of our law-courts, I declare myself to these criminals as their enemy and their accuser, as their pertinacious, bitter, and unrelenting adversary. It is this that I choose, this that I claim, as my duty in my public office, as my duty in that position in which the people of Rome have willed that, from the first day of next January, I should take counsel with them for the public welfare and the punishment of evil men. This is the most splendid and noble spectacle that I can promise to bestow during my aedileship on the people of Rome. I here issue this warning, this public notice, this preliminary proclamation: To all those who are in the habit of depositing or receiving deposits for bribery, of undertaking to offer or offering bribes, or of acting as agents or go-betweens for the corruption of judges in our courts, and to all those who have offered to make use of their power or their shamelessness for these purposes: in this present trial, take care that your hands and your minds are kept clear of this vile crime. . . .

"And now what do you conceive that my feelings will be, if in this very trial I shall find that any offence of this description has been committed? For you must note that I can bring many witnesses to prove that Gaius Verres, when in Sicily, has frequently said, in the presence of many listeners, that he had a powerful friend in whose protection he trusted while plundering the province; and that he was not trying to make money for himself alone, but had those three years of his Sicilian praetorship so parcelled out as to feel he would do well if he might apply the profits of one year to increasing his own fortune, hand over those of the second year to his advocates and defenders, and reserve the whole of the great third year, the richest and most profitable of the three, for his judges.

"**41.** And this suggests to me the repetition of a remark which I made before Manius Glabrio recently when the challenging of judges was taking place, and which I could see made a profound impression upon the people of Rome. I said that I believed the day would come when our foreign subjects would be sending deputations to our people, asking for the repeal of the existing law and the abolition of the Extortion Court. Were there no such Court, they imagine that any one governor would merely carry off what was enough for himself and his family: whereas with the courts as they now are, each governor carries off what will be enough to satisfy himself, his advocates and supporters, and his judges and their president: and this is a wholly unlimited amount. They feel that they may meet the demands of a greedy man's cupidity, but cannot meet those of a guilty man's acquittal.

"**42.** How illustrious are our Courts of Law, how splendid is the reputation of our Order, if the allies of Rome desire the abolition of that very Extortion Court, which our ancestors established for those allies' benefit! Would Verres, indeed, ever have cherished fair hopes for himself, had his mind not been saturated with this foul opinion of you? An opinion that should make him yet more loathsome, if that be possible, to you than to the Roman people, this man who believes you to be as avaricious, as criminal, as false and perjured as he is himself.

"**43.** Now I entreat you, gentlemen, in God's name to take thought, and to devise measures, to meet this state of affairs. I would warn you and solemnly remind you of what is clear to me, that heaven itself has granted you this opportunity of delivering our whole Order from unpopularity and hatred, from dishonour and disgrace. Men reckon that our courts of law have no strictness left, no conscience—nay, by now, no existence worth the name. The result is that we are contemned and despised by the people of Rome. We have been groaning, and that for many years, under a heavy load of infamy.

"**44.** Let me tell you that it was for this reason, and for no other, that the people of Rome have expressed so strong a desire for the restoration of the powers of the tribunes. Their demand for that was but nominally and apparently a demand for the thing itself: their real demand was for honest law-courts. This fact was not missed by that wise and eminent man Quintus Catulus. When our distinguished general Gnaeus Pompeius introduced his measure to restore the powers of the tribunes, Catulus, on being called upon to speak, began his speech with a most impressive declaration, that the members of that House were proving ineffective and immoral guardians of our courts of justice; and that had they only chosen, in their capacity as judges, to maintain the honour of Rome. people would not have felt so acutely their loss of the tribunes' powers.

"**45.** In fact, when Gnaeus Pompeius himself, as consul-elect, for the first time addressed a public meeting near the city, and, in accordance with what appeared to be a very general expectation, declared his intention of restoring the powers of the tribunes, his words elicited a murmuring noise of grateful approval from the assembly: but when he observed, in the course of the same speech, that our provinces had been wasted and laid desolate, that our law-courts were behaving scandalously and wickedly, and that he meant to take steps to deal with this evil—then it was with no mere murmur, but with a mighty roar, that the people of Rome showed their satisfaction.

"**46.** To-day the eyes of the world are upon us, waiting to see how far the conduct of each man among us will be marked by obedience to his conscience and by observance of the law. It is noted that since the passage of the tribunician law a single senator, a man of quite slender means, has been condemned; an act which, though not censured, nevertheless affords no great room for commendation, for integrity cannot be commendable where no man has either the power or the will to corrupt it.

"**47.** It is the present trial in which, even as you will pass your verdict upon the prisoner, so the people of Rome will pass its verdict upon yourselves. It is this man's case that will determine whether, with a court composed of Senators, the condemnation of a very guilty and very rich man can possibly occur.

"And further, the prisoner is such that he is distinguished by nothing except his monstrous offences and immense wealth: if, therefore, he is acquitted, it will be impossible to imagine any explanation but the most shameful; it will not appear that there has been any liking for him, any family bond, any record of other and better actions, no, nor even any moderation in some one vice, that could palliate the number and enormity of his vicious deeds.

"**48.** And lastly, gentlemen, I shall so handle this case, I shall put before you facts of such a kind—so notorious, so well corroborated by evidence, so sweeping, and so convincing—that nobody will seek to urge you to acquit this man as a personal favour. I have a definite plan of procedure by which to unearth and set my hands upon all the intrigues of him and his friends; and I shall deal with this business in such a fashion that all their stratagems will seem to stand revealed, not merely to men's ears, but to the very eyes of the people of this country.

"**49.** You have the power of removing and destroying the dishonour and the disgrace that have for several years past attached to this our Order. It is admitted upon all hands that, since these Courts were first constituted in their present shape, no body of judges has assembled of equal eminence and equal distinction. If this body of judges shall in any way come to grief, the universal opinion will be, that for the administration of justice we must seek, not fitter men from the same Order, for none such could be found, but some other Order altogether.

"**50.** And therefore, gentlemen, in the first place, I pray Heaven to justify the confidence I feel, that no man in this Court will be detected in evil-doing, save that one man whose evil-doing has been long since discovered; and in the next place I declare to you, and, gentlemen, I declare to the people of Rome, that if other evil-doers there shall be, I will, so God help me, sooner lose my life than lose the vigour and the resolution that shall secure their punishment for the evil they have done. . . .

"**53.** I am firmly resolved to prevent our having a change of president or judges for the case before us. I will not allow the decision to be delayed to a time when men who, by a gross innovation, have been collectively summoned before a consul-elect by his servants, and who as yet have refused to go, may be ordered before a consul in office by his constables: to a time when those unhappy persons, who were once the allies and friends of Rome, but now are slaves and suppliants, will not only be deprived, through these men's official power, of their rights and their whole fortunes, but will be denied even the opportunity of remonstrating about their loss.

"**54.** Assuredly I will not suffer the reply to our case to be made only when forty days have passed after I have ended my speech for the prosecution, and the lapse of time has blurred the memory of the charges we bring. I will not permit the settlement of this case to be delayed until after the departure from Rome of these multitudes that have simultaneously assembled, from all parts of Italy, to attend the elections, the games, and the census. As, in this trial, it is for you to reap the reward of popularity and risk the danger of disapproval, and for us to face the toil and anxiety involved; so, I hold, it is for all men to be admitted to the knowledge of what shall here take place, and to record in their memories the words that each speaker shall utter.

"**55.** My calling of my witnesses at once will be no novelty; that has been done before, and by men who now hold leading positions in the country. The novelty that you will note, gentlemen, is this: I shall so deal with the evidence of my witnesses as first to state each charge in full, and after supporting it by questioning, argument, and comment, then to bring forward my witnesses to that particular charge. There will thus be no difference between the usual method of prosecution and this new one of mine, except that in the former the witnesses are not called until all the speeches are over, whereas in the latter they will be called with reference to each charge in turn: so that, further, our opponents will have the same facilities as ourselves for questions, arguments, and comments. If there is anyone who regrets the absence of the continuous speech for the prosecution, he shall hear it in the second part of the trial: for the moment he must see that our line of action, being directed to thwarting, by rational means, the trickery of our adversaries, is the only one possible.

"**56.** The scope of the prosecution in the first part of the trial will be this: . . .

"**139.** I have now done enough for the people of Sicily, enough to meet the claims of my friendship for them, and to carry out the promise I made them. What still remains of my case, gentlemen, is something not taken upon me but born in me; something not brought to me from without, but indissolubly entwined with the inmost roots and fibres of my being. It is no longer a question of the preservation of our allies: it is a question of the life and existence of Roman citizens, or in other words, of each and every one of ourselves.

"Gentlemen, do not look for me to prove my statements in this matter, as though some part of them were open to doubt: all the facts I shall give you will be so notorious that I might have been making all Sicily a witness to their truth.

"The madness that accompanies unscrupulous wickedness plunged this man's unbridled passions and savage heart into such a depth of insanity that he never hesitated, in the open sight of our countrymen, to produce the punishments devised for convicted slaves and inflict them on citizens of Rome.

"**140.** Need I remind you how many he had flogged? Gentlemen, the simple fact is this: when Verres was governor of Sicily, no distinction whatsoever was made, in this respect, between Roman citizens and other people.

"And the result of this practice was that before long his lictors were in the habit of actually laying hands upon the persons of Roman citizens without so much as waiting for his orders.—

"Can you deny this, Verres—that in the market-place of Lilybaeum, where there is a large Roman community, an elderly business man named Gaius Servilius, a Roman citizen belonging to the Panhormus community, was beaten with rods before your judgement-seat till he fell to the ground at your feet? Deny this first charge if you can: all Lilybaeum saw it, and all Sicily heard of it. My charge is that a Roman citizen was beaten by your lictors till he collapsed fainting before your eyes.

"141. And, God help us, for what a reason!—Though indeed it is to the detriment of our common interest, and of our status as citizens, that I ask what the reason was in the case of Servilius, as if there were any possible reason that could justify such a thing's befalling any Roman citizen whatsoever. Forgive me, gentlemen, in this one instance: in the others I shall not spend long in asking what the reasons were. Servilius had talked rather freely about Verres' rascality and wickedness. . . .

"142. In the midst of his appeal he was surrounded by six lictors, muscular fellows who had had plenty of practice in assaulting and flogging people, and who now proceeded to beat him savagely with rods; till finally the senior lictor Sextius, a man whom I have already often mentioned, took the butt end of his stick, and began to strike the poor man violently across the eyes, so that he fell helpless to the ground, his face and eyes streaming with blood. . . . Such was the treatment he then received; and having been carried off for dead at the time, very soon afterwards he died. . . .

"143. Of the tortures inflicted on other Roman citizens I might well speak in general and comprehensive terms, instead of taking them one by one. While Verres was governor, the prison constructed at Syracuse by the cruel tyrant Dionysius, and known as the Stone Quarries, was the permanent home of Roman citizens.

"Let the thought or the sight of any one of them annoy him, and the man was flung into the Quarries forthwith.

"I perceive, gentlemen, the indignation which this arouses in you all; and I observed the same thing, in the first part of the trial, when the facts were being stated by witnesses. You hold, of course, that it is not only here in Rome that we should be sure of enjoying the freedom that is our right: not only where we have the tribunes of the people, the other officers of state, the courts of law that crowd our Forum, the authority of our Senate, the public opinion of the assembled people of Rome. No: the infringement of a Roman citizen's rights, in whatsoever land, and among whatsoever people, is a thing which in your judgement affects the freedom and dignity of all Roman citizens alike.

"**144.** In that place where foreign criminals and scoundrels, where pirates and public enemies are confined, how could you dare, Verres, to imprison that multitude of Roman citizens? Did no thought of your trial ever enter your mind? no thought of your assembled countrymen? no thought of the great company now met together, now contemplating you with angry and hostile eyes? Even at that distance, did the greatness of the Roman people, did the actual picture of this crowded gathering never present itself to your eyes or your imagination? Did you suppose that you would never return to the place where they could see you, never re-enter the forum of the Roman nation, never become subject to the authority of our laws and our courts of law? . . .

"**145.** Now what gave rise to this display of wanton cruelty, and caused the man to load himself with so heavy a burden of crimes? Gentlemen, it was simply a special new device for securing plunder. . . . Every ship that arrived from Asia or Syria, from Tyre or Alexandria, was promptly seized by his special band of spies and watchmen: the voyagers were all flung into the Stone Quarries, the cargoes and merchandise were carried off to the governor's residence. . . .

"**146.** And what reason for this abominable cruelty was put forward by Verres at the time? The same, gentlemen, as that which will be brought up by his advocates now.

"All persons who landed in Sicily with any considerable store of goods he denounced as belonging to the army of Sertorius and being fugitives from Dianium.

"They sought to escape his anger by exhibiting their wares—Tyrian purple, incense and perfumes and linen fabrics, jewels and pearls, Greek wines, Asiatic slaves—so as to prove by the nature of their cargoes from what part of the world they had come.

"They did not foresee that the things they hoped would prove their innocence and save them were just the things that would lead to their ruin. Verres declared that they had acquired these goods by having dealings with the pirates, ordered them to be marched off to the Stone Quarries, and took their ships and cargoes into careful custody.

"**147.** These methods presently crowded the prison with honest traders; and then those things began to happen of which you have heard from Lucius Suettius, a Roman knight and most excellent man, and of which you shall hear from the others likewise. There, in that prison, guiltless Roman citizens were most shamefully strangled. Now at last the cry 'I am a Roman citizen,' the famous appeal that has so often brought men help and rescue among savage races in the furthest corners of the earth, was to hasten the infliction and increase the agony of these men's death.—

"Well, Verres? what answer to this charge are you contemplating? not, I presume, that I am lying, or inventing, or exaggerating? you will hardly venture to make any such suggestion as those to your advocates here?—Let us have, if you please, out of his own special treasures a Syracusan document that he thinks of as composed according to his own wishes; let us have the prison record, which is carefully kept so as to show the dates on which prisoners are received, and on which they die—or are put to death. . . .

"149. If it were some king, or foreign community, or savage tribe, that had behaved thus to Roman citizens, should we not as a nation be taking steps to punish the offenders, and sending our armies against them? could we be suffering such an insult, such a blot on the honour of Rome, without exacting vengeance and retribution? In how many great wars, think you, did our ancestors engage, because Rome's citizens were alleged to have been insulted, her seamen arrested, her merchants robbed?

"Yet I am not now complaining that these men were arrested, nor feeling it intolerable that they were robbed; my charge is that, after being deprived of ships and slaves and merchandise, honest merchants were flung into prison, and in that prison, being Roman citizens, were put to death.

"150. If I were addressing an audience of Scythians, instead of speaking here in Rome to this vast gathering of Romans, in the hearing of a body of those Senators who are Rome's most distinguished citizens, in the Forum of the Roman nation, about the cruel execution of that multitude of Roman citizens—even so my words would be arousing indignation, even in those barbarian souls; for so glorious is our great empire, so highly is the name of Rome honoured in all the world, that it is felt to be beyond the power of any man to treat our countrymen with cruelty such as this. . . .

"156. What shall be said of those who were led forth in large numbers to be executed, among the captured pirates, with their heads covered?—What is the meaning of this novel precaution of yours, and what made you devise it? Can it be that you were shaken by the cries of distress that your treatment of Herennius drew from Flavius and the others? Or was it the deep respect felt for the strong character and high standing of Marcus Annius that made you a little less careless and reckless than usual? I mean the Annius who a day or two ago testified on oath that a man who was no casual foreigner just come from abroad, but a Roman citizen born at Syracuse and known to all the Roman citizens in Syracuse, was beheaded by your orders.—

"157. After those men's outcry, after that outrage had become known to and resented by everyone, Verres proceeded to execute his victims not indeed less brutally than before, but more cautiously.

"He took to having his Roman citizens led forth to die with their heads covered, while having them nevertheless put to death in public because the people in that district, as I have already told you, were making an inconveniently careful estimate of the number of pirates missing.—

"Was this the treatment decreed for honest Romans, when you were governor of Sicily? was this the prospect that their occupation afforded them? was this all the respect in which their rights and their lives were held? Are the perils and accidents that all traders must inevitably face so sadly few that such further terrors as these must threaten them, in Roman provinces and at the hands of Roman governors?—

"To what end has Sicily been our near neighbour and loyal dependency, the home of our faithful allies and our honoured countrymen? to what end has she always gladly welcomed every citizen of Rome who would dwell within her borders? Has it been only for this, that men who were sailing back from the furthest coasts of Syria and Egypt, whose Roman dress had procured them no small measure of honour even among barbarous peoples, who had escaped the clutches of lurking pirates and the perils of storm and tempest, should fall slain by the headsman's axe in Sicily when they felt themselves already safe at home?

"158. And now, gentlemen, I am to speak of Publius Gavius, burgess of Consa; and with what strength of voice, what weight of eloquence, what sorrow of heart must my words be spoken! Nay, of sorrow, indeed, my heart has no lack; rather it is voice and eloquence wherewith I must strive to equip myself in a measure befitting my theme and the sorrow that I feel. Such is the charge I now bring that when I was first told of the facts I could not see myself making use of them; aware though I was of their complete truth, I could not imagine that they would be believed. Constrained by the tearful entreaties of all the Roman citizens who are business men in Sicily, and encouraged by the testimony of the worthy inhabitants of Vibo, and by that of the whole population of Regium, and by that of a number of Roman knights who as it happened were at the time in Messana, in the first part of this trial I called no more witnesses than might suffice to convince everyone of the facts.

"**159.** What am I to do now? Hour after hour I have been handling the single topic of Verres' abominable cruelty. In speaking of other instances of that cruelty, I have almost wholly exhausted the resources of such language as befits his wickedness, and have not taken steps to keep your attention awake by varying the nature of my charges. And how, therefore, shall I deal with this terrible affair?

"There is, I think, but one course, one method possible. I will put the bare facts before you. They speak so forcibly for themselves that there is no need of eloquence, from my own feeble lips or from the lips of anyone else, to kindle your indignation.

"**160.** The man of whom I speak, Gavius of Consa, was one of those Roman citizens whom Verres threw into prison. Somehow or other he escaped from the Stone Quarries, and made his way to Messana. Italy was now visible only a few miles away, and the walls of Regium with its population of Roman citizens; he had come forth from the awful shadow of death, revived and strengthened by the light of freedom and the fresh air of justice; and so he began to talk indignantly to people in Messana of how he, a Roman citizen, had been thrown into prison, and how he was going straight to Rome and would be ready for Verres on his arrival there.

"The poor fellow was not aware that to say such things in Messana was equivalent to saying them to the governor in his own house; for Verres, as I have already explained, had chosen this town to assist him in his crimes, to receive his stolen goods, and to share the secret of all his abominable deeds.

"The result was that Gavius was at once seized and taken before the chief magistrate of Messana. Verres chanced to arrive there that same day, and it was reported to him that there was a Roman citizen with an angry story about having been in the Stone Quarries at Syracuse, who was already going aboard a ship, uttering unpleasantly savage threats against Verres, when they had dragged him ashore again and kept him in custody for Verres to deal with as he thought best.

"**161.** Verres thanked these people, commending warmly their kind and careful attention to his interests.

"Then he made for the market-place, on fire with mad and wicked rage, his eyes blazing, and cruelty showing clearly in every feature of his face. Everyone was wondering how far he would go and what he was meaning to do, when he suddenly ordered the man to be flung down, stripped naked and tied up in the open market-place, and rods to be got ready.

"The unhappy man cried out that he was a Roman citizen, a burgess of Consa; that he had served in the army under the distinguished Roman knight Lucius Raecius, who was in business at Panhormus and could assure Verres of the truth of his story.

"To this Verres replied that he had discovered that Gavius had been sent to Sicily as a spy by the leaders of the fugitive army, a charge which was brought by no informer, for which there was no evidence, and which nobody saw any reason to believe. He then ordered the man to be flogged severely all over his body.

"**162.** There in the open market-place of Messana a Roman citizen, gentlemen, was beaten with rods; and all the while, amid the crack of the falling blows, no groan was heard from the unhappy man, no words came from his lips in his agony except 'I am a Roman citizen.' By thus proclaiming his citizenship he had been hoping to avert all those blows and shield his body from torture; yet not only did he fail to secure escape from those cruel rods, but when he persisted in his entreaties and his appeals to his citizen rights, a cross was made ready—yes, a cross, for that hapless and broken sufferer, who had never seen such an accursed thing till then.

"**163.** Does freedom, that precious thing, mean nothing? nor the proud privileges of a citizen of Rome? nor the law of Porcius, the laws of Sempronius? nor the tribunes' power, whose loss our people felt so deeply till now at last it has been restored to them? Have all these things come in the end to mean so little that in a Roman province, in a town whose people have special privileges, a Roman citizen could be bound and flogged in the market-place by a man who owed his rods and axes to the favour of the Roman people?

"When the fire and hot metal plates and the like were brought to torture him, even if his agonized entreaties, his pitiful cries could not stay your hand, was your soul untouched even by the tears and the loud groans of the Roman citizens who then stood by?

"You dared to crucify any living man who claimed to be a Roman citizen?—Gentlemen, in the earlier part of this trial I refrained from speaking of this matter with my present vehemence; and I did so because, as you could see, the minds of the audience were being strongly excited against Verres by feelings of distress, of hatred, of fear for the general safety.

"I deliberately kept within bounds, on that occasion, both my own utterances and the evidence of Gaius Numitorius, the eminent Roman knight whom I called as a witness; and I was glad that Glabrio did what it was very wise for him to do—abruptly adjourn the sitting while the witness was still speaking.

"The truth being that he was afraid that men might see the people of Rome forcibly inflicting upon Verres the retribution which it feared he would escape at the hands of the law and of yourselves as his judges.

"**164.** But since it has now been made quite plain to everyone, Verres, how your case is going and what the result for you will be, I will deal thus with you.

"You declare all of a sudden that Gavius had been a spy. Well, I will prove that you had thrown him into prison in the Stone Quarries at Syracuse. And I will not prove this merely by quoting the Syracusan prison records: you shall not be able to say that I found the name Gavius in those records, and then selected it so as to be able to make a fictitious identification of this Gavius with the other. No, I will call witnesses, out of whom you shall make your choice, to testify that this man and no other was thrown into the Quarries at Syracuse by you.

"I will also put forward fellow-townsmen and intimate friends of his from Consa, who will show you and your judges, too late for you but not for them, that the Publius Gavius whom you crucified was a Roman citizen and a burgess of Consa, and not a spy from the ranks of the fugitives.

"**165.** Now when I have given your friends and supporters ample proof of all these facts that I undertake to prove, I intend to lay hold of the very point which you yourself concede me, and proclaim myself content with that. What did you say yourself the other day, when you leapt up terrified by the shouts and angry gestures of your country-men—what did you tell us plainly then? That the man kept calling out that he was a Roman citizen simply in order to delay his execution, but was in fact a mere spy.

"Very well then, my witnesses are telling the truth. It is precisely this that we are told by Gaius Numitorius, by those two well-known gentlemen Marcus and Publius Cottius who come from the Tauro-menium district, by Quintus Lucceius who has been an important banker in Regium. . . . For until now the witnesses I have called have been chosen not from among those who were to state that they knew

Gavius personally, but from those who were to state that they saw him when he was being dragged off to be crucified in spite of his proclaiming himself a Roman citizen.

"This is exactly what you, Verres, say, this is what you admit, that he kept proclaiming himself a Roman citizen, that this mention of his citizenship had not even so much effect upon you as to produce a little hesitation, or to delay, even for a little, the infliction of that cruel and disgusting penalty.—

"166. Of this admission, gentlemen, I lay hold, I stand by this, I am content with this one thing, all the rest may pass unheeded: his own admission must inevitably ensnare him and put the knife to his throat.—You did not know who he was, you had reasons for believing him a spy? I do not ask you what those reasons were. Out of your own mouth I accuse you: the man claimed to be a Roman citizen.

"If you, Verres, had been made prisoner in Persia or the remotest part of India, and were being dragged off to execution, what cry would you be uttering, save that you were a Roman citizen? You, a stranger among strangers, among savages, among a people inhabiting the farthest and remotest regions of the earth, would have been well served by your claim to that citizenship whose glory is known throughout the world: what, then, of this man whom you were hurrying to execution? whoever he was, he was unknown to you, and he declared himself a Roman citizen: could not that statement, that claim of citizenship, secure from you on your judgement-seat if not remission yet at least postponement of the sentence of death?

"167. Poor men of humble birth sail across the seas to shores they have never seen before, where they find themselves among strangers, and cannot always have with them acquaintances to vouch for them. Yet such trust have they in the single fact of their citizenship that they count on being safe, not only where they find our magistrates, who are restrained by the fear of law and public opinion, and not only among their own countrymen, to whom they are bound by the ties of a common language and civic rights and much else beside: no, wherever they find themselves, they feel confident that this one fact will be their defence.

"168. Take away this confidence, take away this defence from Roman citizens; lay it down that to cry 'I am a Roman citizen' shall help no man at all; make it possible for governors and other persons to inflict upon a man who declares himself a Roman citizen any cruel penalty they choose, on the plea that they do not know who the man is; do this, accept that plea, and forthwith you exclude Roman citizens from all our provinces, from all foreign kingdoms and republics, from every region of that great world to which Romans, above all other men, have always had free access until now.

"And then again, when Gavius named the Roman knight Lucius Raecius, who was in Sicily at the time—might you not at least have written to him at Panhormus? Your Messanian friends would have kept your man in safe custody, you would have had him chained and locked up, till Raecius arrived from Panhormus. Should he identify the man, you would no doubt lessen the extreme severity of the sentence: should he fail to do so, then you would be free to set up this precedent, if you chose, that a man who was not known to yourself, and could not produce some person of substance to vouch for him, might be put to death on the cross, even if he were a Roman citizen.

"**169.** But I need say no more about Gavius. It was not Gavius against whom your hate was then displayed: you declared war upon the whole principle of the rights of the Roman citizen body. You were the enemy, I say again, not of that individual man, but of the common liberties of us all.

"What else was the meaning of your order to the Messanians, who had followed their regular custom by setting up the cross on the Pompeian Road behind the town, to set it up in the part of the town that looks over the Straits? and why did you add words that you cannot possibly deny having used, words that you said openly in the hearing of all—that you purposely chose this spot to give this man, since he claimed to be a Roman citizen, a view of Italy and a prospect of his home country as he hung on his cross? That is the only cross, gentlemen, ever set up in this spot in all Messana's history; and you now see why. This place with its view of Italy was deliberately picked out by Verres, that his victim, as he died in pain and agony, might feel how yonder narrow channel marked the frontier between the land of slavery and the land of freedom, and that Italy might see her son, as he hung there, suffer the worst extreme of the tortures inflicted upon slaves.

"**170.** To bind a Roman citizen is a crime, to flog him is an abomination, to slay him is almost an act of murder: to crucify him is—what? There is no fitting word that can possibly describe so horrible a deed. Not satisfied with all the cruelty I have told you of, 'Let him be in sight of his native land,' he cries, 'let him die with justice and freedom before his eyes.' It was not Gavius, not one obscure man, [a Roman citizen,] whom you nailed upon that cross of agony: it was the universal principle that Romans are free men.—

"Nay, do but mark the villain's shamelessness! One can imagine how it vexed him to be unable to set up that cross to crucify us Roman citizens in our Forum, in our place of public assembly and public speech: for he picked out the corner of his province that should be most like Rome in its populousness, and nearest to Rome in its position; he would have this memorial of his abandoned wickedness stand in sight of Italy, at the entrance-gate of Sicily, in a place where all who came or went that way by sea must pass close by it.

"**171.** If I were not speaking to Roman citizens; not to men who are our country's friends; not to those who have heard of the name and fame of Rome; not even to human beings, but to brute beasts; nay, to go even further, if I were minded to tell this tale of suffering and wrong to the stones and rocks of some lonely desert waste, cruelty and injustice so awful as this would rouse sympathy even in the world of mute and lifeless things. And since those whom I am in fact addressing are senators of Rome, main pillars of our laws and our law-courts and our civic rights, I may rest assured that Verres will be pronounced the one Roman citizen for whom that cross would be a fitting punishment, and no others deserving, even in the smallest degree, of being treated thus.

"**172.** A little while ago, gentlemen, the pitiful fate of those innocent ship's captains was bringing the tears into our eyes. It was right and proper for us to be affected thus deeply by the anguish of our guiltless allies: how must we be affected now, when we hear of the anguish of our own kinsman?

"I say our kinsman, for we must recognize blood-kinship between all Roman citizens; truth, not less than concern for the general safety, bids us do so. And now in this place all the citizens of Rome, all those who are here and all who are elsewhere, are looking to you to do strict justice, appealing to your honour, imploring your help. They believe that their every right and interest and advantage, yes, that the whole of their liberty, depends on the verdict that you are to give."

ROME VERSUS CHRISTIANITY
PILATE THE ROMAN GOVERNOR CONDEMNS CHRIST THE SON OF GOD TO THE CROSS

Pilate therefore again went outside and said to them, "Behold, I bring him out to you, that you may know that I find no guilt in him." Jesus therefore came forth, wearing the crown of thorns and the purple cloak. And he said to them, "Behold the man!" When, therefore, the chief priests and the attendants saw him, they cried out, saying, "Crucify him! Crucify him!" Pilate said to them, "Take him yourselves and crucify him, for I find no guilt in him." The Jews answered him, "We have a Law, and according to that Law he must die, because he has made himself Son of God."

Now when Pilate heard this statement, he feared the more. And he again went back into the governor's hall, and said to Jesus, "Where art thou from?" But Jesus gave him no answer. Pilate therefore said to him, "Dost thou not speak to me? Dost thou not know that I have power to crucify thee, and that I have power to release thee?" Jesus answered, "Thou wouldst have no power at all over me were it not given thee from above. Therefore, he who betrayed me to thee has the greater sin."

And from then on Pilate was looking for a way to release him. But the Jews cried out, saying, "If thou release this man, thou art no friend of Caesar; for everyone who makes himself king speaks against Caesar."

Pilate therefore, when he heard these words, brought Jesus outside, and sat down on the judgment-seat, at a place called Lithostrotos, but in Hebrew, Gabbatha. Now it was the day of preparation for the Pasch, about the sixth hour.[1] And he said to the Jews, "Behold your king!" But they cried out, "Away with him! Away with him! Crucify him!" Pilate said to them, "Shall I crucify your king?" The chief priests answered, "We have no king but Caesar." Then he handed him over to them to be crucified (John 19:4-16).

---

[1] According to Scriptural calculation of time, the day is divided roughly into four periods, called the third hour, the sixth hour, and so forth. Each period embraces *three* hours of our time, the "third hour" beginning at nine in the morning. Thus noon of our time might be called either "about the third hour" or "about the sixth hour" in Roman time.

POPE PETER DEFIES THE AUTHORITY
OF THE JEWS

But the chief priest and his party came and they called together the Sanhedrin and all the elders of the children of Israel, and sent to the prison to have them brought. . . . And having brought them, they set them before the Sanhedrin. And the high priest questioned them, saying, "We strictly charged you not to teach in this name, and behold, you have filled Jerusalem with your teaching, and want to bring this man's blood upon us."

But Peter and the apostles answered and said, "We must obey God rather than men" (Acts 5:21, 27-29).

PAUL APPEALS TO HIS RIGHTS AS A
ROMAN CITIZEN

Paul said to the centurion who was standing by, "Is it legal for you to scourge a Roman, and him uncondemned?" When the centurion heard this, he went to the tribune and reported, saying, "What art thou about to do? This man is a Roman citizen." Then the tribune came and said to him, "Tell me, art thou a Roman?" And he said, "Yes." And the tribune answered, "I obtained this citizenship at a great price." And Paul said, "But I am a citizen by birth." Straightway therefore those who had been going to torture him left him; and the tribune himself was alarmed to ascertain that Paul was a Roman citizen, and that he had bound him (Acts 22:25-29).

PAUL APPEALS TO CAESAR

And the next day he [Festus] took his seat on the tribunal and ordered Paul brought in. And when he was fetched, the Jews who had come down from Jerusalem surrounded him and brought many serious charges against him, which they were unable to prove. Paul said in his own defense, "Neither against the Law of the Jews nor against the temple nor against Caesar have I committed any offense."

But Festus, wishing to do the Jews a favor, answered Paul and said, "Art thou willing to go up to Jerusalem and be tried there before me on these charges?" But Paul said, "I am standing at the tribunal of Caesar; there I ought to be tried. To Jews I have done no wrong, as thou thyself very well knowest. For if I have done any wrong or committed a crime deserving of death, I do not refuse to die. But if there is no ground to their charges against me, no one can give me up to them; I appeal to Caesar." Then Festus, after conferring with the council, answered, "Thou hast appealed to Caesar; to Caesar thou shalt go" (Acts 25:6-12).

PETER AND PAUL MARTYRED AT ROME

Peter and Paul, entreat ye . . .

O fortunate Rome, you are made sacred by the glorious blood of the two princes! Incarnadined by their [streaming] blood you surpass all the other beauties of the world.

MARTYRDOM UNDER THE EMPERORS

On another day, when we were eating breakfast, we were suddenly seized for a hearing, and came to the forum. The report (of our seizure) immediately ran abroad through the neighboring parts of the forum, and a large crowd gathered. We climbed upon the platform. The others when questioned confessed. My turn came. There appeared on the spot my father together with my son; he drew me down from the steps with these words: "Offer sacrifice, have pity on the child." And Hilarianus the revenue collector, who then held the power of pronouncing capital sentence in place of Minucius Timinianus the proconsul, who had died, said: "Spare the grey hairs of your father; spare the infancy of your child. Offer sacrifice for the Emperors' welfare." And I made reply: "I am not doing it." And Hilarianus said: "You are a Christian?" And I answered: "I am a Christian." . . . Then he passed sentence upon all of us, and condemned us to the beasts, and we go down into the dungeon joyfully.

The day of their victory dawned and they marched from the dungeon into the amphitheater as if they were about to enter heaven. . . . "Stand fast in your faith, love one another all of you and be not scandalized in our sufferings."

CYPRIAN THE BISHOP BEARS WITNESS
UNTO BLOOD

Galerius Maximus the proconsul said to Cyprian the bishop: "Are you Thascius Cyprian?" Cyprian the bishop answered: "I am." Proconsul Galerius Maximus said: "Have you paraded before men as a bishop of impious mind?" Bishop Cyprian answered: "I have." Proconsul Galerius Maximus said: "They have given you orders to offer sacrifice to the most holy emperors." Bishop Cyprian answered: "I am not doing it." Said Galerius Maximus: "Look to your interests." Bishop

Cyprian replied: "Do what has been commanded you; in a matter as just as this there is no room for reconsideration of one's interests."

Galerius Maximus conferred with the council and pronounced sentence with great difficulty in words of this sort: "You have for a long time lived with an impious attitude, and have drawn to you many men of a wicked conspiracy. You have set yourself up an enemy to the Roman gods and sacred practices. The pious and most sacred rulers Valerius, Gallienus the son of Augustus, and the most noble Caesar Valerian have been unable to recall you to the observance of their sacred rites and therefore, since you are the instigator of the most wicked crimes and have been arrested as their leader, you shall yourself be an example to those men whom you have linked with you in your crime; in your blood will obedience be established." With these words he read aloud the sentence from the record: "It is decreed that Thascius Cyprian be punished with death." Bishop Cyprian said: "Thanks be to God."

"LICET CHRISTIANOS ESSE"—CONSTANTINE

When happily both I, Constantine Augustus, and I, Licinius Augustus, had met at Milan and were holding under consideration everything which has to do with public convenience and security, those things—among others which we saw would profit the majority—we believed had to be regulated in an especial manner, in which the worship of God was involved, that so we might give to Christians and to all men the free power of following the religion which each one desired, so that the divinity may indeed be able to exist in his heavenly seat placated and well-disposed toward us and toward all men who have been placed under our power. And so we believed that we had to enter upon this according to beneficial counsel and right reason, namely that we should think permission must be denied to no one at all who had given his mind over either to the observance of the Christians or to that religion which he felt was most fitted to himself, so that the most high divinity, to whose religion we submit ourselves with freedom of heart, may show us in all things his usual favor and good will.

ROME—THE CAPITAL OF CHRISTENDOM

O noble Rome, mistress of the world, of all cities most excellent, red with the rosy blood of martyrs, gleaming with the white lilies of virgins, we salute thee, we bless thee in all things: hail through the ages!

ST. AMBROSE DEFIES THE EMPEROR

Tribute is Caesar's; it is not denied him. The Church is God's. It must surely not be given to Caesar, because the temple of God cannot be Caesar's jurisdiction. No one can deny that this is said with due respect for the emperor's honor. For what can be more honorable than that the emperor be spoken of as a son of the Church? When this is said, it is said without fault; it is said with favor. For the emperor is within the Church, not above the Church; a good emperor seeks to help the Church (and) does not oppose it.

THE POPES TODAY—WORLD LEADERS

"An invention finally which rejects and denies the rights, dignity, and freedom of the human person."

"This is not the place, most eminent prelates, this is not the time to follow (in detail) the single things which our lamented Pope did so remarkably. But, since it falls to my lot, at your bidding and command, to say a few words about his long and glorious pontificate, I shall strive to recall under one large heading the main part of his apostolic office, that part namely which is peculiarly related to his teachings as taken from his encyclical letters, which were written with a view to persuading and nourishing peace of mind and heart, peace in the home and state, peace among all peoples and tribes, according to that famous sign: *The Peace of Christ in the Kingdom of Christ.*"

TO THE ENTIRE FAMILY OF MANKIND
ANXIOUS AMID SO MUCH DISCORD AND GRIEF,
WITH JUSTICE AS A LEADER, AND UNDER THE
AUSPICES OF CHARITY,
WITH THE HEART OF A FATHER HE URGED
BROTHERLY HARMONY.

I BRING YOU TIDINGS OF GREAT JOY.
WE HAVE FOR POPE
THE MOST EMINENT AND REVEREND CARDINAL
EUGENIO PACELLI
WHO HAS ASSUMED THE NAME OF
PIUS XII.

"And we wish to add to this fatherly message of Ours a sign of, and an invitation to, peace. We speak of that peace which Our predecessor of pious memory urged so earnestly upon men and implored with such eager prayers that he freely offered his life to God for the sake of gaining concord among men; of that peace, the most beautiful gift of God, which surpasses all understanding; of that peace, finally, which arises from justice and charity. We exhort all to that peace which revives souls joined together in the friendship of God and which regulates and composes domestic life in the sacred love of Jesus Christ; to that peace which unites nations and peoples through the mutual interchange of brotherly help; to that peace, finally, and to that concord which must so be re-established among the nations that every race, with the favor and help of God, will by mutual consent, by friendly agreement, and with helpful effort strive for the progress and happiness of the entire family of mankind."

TWO STANDARDS

On the fourth day a meditation will be made on the two standards, the one of Jesus Christ our supreme leader, the other of Lucifer, mankind's chief enemy. . . . There will be a consideration of Christ on the one hand, of Lucifer on the other, each of whom calls all men unto him, to assemble under his banner.

EPILOGUE

The blood of martyrs is the seed of Christians.

EXERCISES BASED ON CICERO

Lesson 1

Exercise 1.—1. Who was Catiline and where was he? 2. Cicero is coming into the Senate, is he not? 3. The Roman people surely do not understand all about it? 4. Who had pointed out each one of us for assassination? 5. Did the consul understand that the conspiracy was already checked by the knowledge of all? 6. For how long had the consul seen that a conspiracy had been formed? 7. The consuls saw it, the Senate understood it, and yet that fellow was still living; he actually came into the Senate; he was noting down and pointing out each of them for assassination. 8. What did you do last night? 9. When, pray tell me, will good times come? 10. The watches of the city do not impress me. 11. The consul saw Catiline's madness. 12. Do you live in the city or not? 13. Good men often shun public places and assemblies. 14. In a night attack they took the fortified city. 15. Where will you go? 16. How long have you lived in this city? 17. Now, in truth, what is that life of yours? 18. What friends have you called together? 19. What are you doing? 20. We all overlook and will overlook many things. 21. The gates of the city were open. 22. Or can we avoid all evils? 23. That ruin which you have long been preparing for all of us should long ago have been visited upon you. 24. The consuls, brave men that they were, had long been shunning Catiline's rage and weapons. 25. Catiline should long ago have been led to death by the consul's order. 26. We have long been avoiding [exciting] the fear of the people. 27. They had long been fortifying the place for holding the Senate. 28. Night before last I saw the consuls in the Senate. 29. What did you see in the city? We saw the conflagration of the Senate. 30. The general perceived that his plans were exposed. 31. Do you think our city is beautiful or not? 32. Surely the Roman people perceived that the city was fortified by garrisons and night watches? 33. With whom did they come into the Senate? 34. With whom do you live in the city? 35. Christ had patience even unto the end. 36. The effrontery and madness of the enemy moved our men even to flight. 37. The enemy had long been desiring the conflagration of the city.

Exercise 2.—Answer in Latin. 1. Who are you? 2. Where do you live? 3. What did you do last night? 4. At what time did you come to this place? 5. With whom did you come? 6. Do you live in the city?

7. Who was Cicero? 8. Cicero became consul, didn't he? 9. He had not seen everything, had he? 10. At what time did he perceive that a conspiracy had been formed? 11. How long has he lived in the city? 12. Where did he summon the Senate? 13. Was the place for holding the Senate fortified? 14. Catiline did not understand everything, did he? 15. Was Catiline aware that his plans were exposed? 16. Was Catiline's character good? 17. The Senate and the Roman people were not unaware of everything, were they? 18. To what end had the conspiracy been formed? 19. Catiline was moved by the fear of all good men, wasn't he? 20. Was Cicero a good man? 21. Do you understand all this? 22. Are we all in the city?

Exercise 3.—1. Ubi vīvis? 2. Nōnne in urbe vīvis? 3. Quam diū in urbe vīvēs? 4. Num populus furōrem Catilīnae intellēxit? 5. Intellēxitne jam Cicerō omnia? 6. Quō tempore Cicerō in senātum vēnit? 7. Quibuscum vēnit? 8. Quōs eā nocte Catilīna convocāvit? 9. At ubi cōnsulēs erant? 10. Nōnne haec omnia vērō intellegitis? 11. Populus Rōmānus audāciam Catilīnae ignōrāvit. 12. Proximā nocte vēnērunt. 13. Tempora bona nunc veniunt. 14. Quō tempore venient? 15. Id vērō ignōrō. 16. Superiōre nocte vigiliās senātūs vidī. 17. Portae urbis patent et ignem vidērunt. 18. Jam prīdem Cicerō locum habendī senātūs mūniēbat. 19. Quō hostēs fugient? 20. Num senātum in urbe continēbit? 21. Nōnne conjūrātiōnem patēre arbitrāris? 22. Utrum intellēxit populus Rōmānus haec omnia an ignōrāvit? 23. Sānctī scientiam Deī usque ad fīnem vītae student. 24. Ad mortem tē ducī jam prīdem oportēbat. 25. Jam dūdum pestem vītāmus. 26. Nōnne intellegis cōnsulem conjūrātiōnem tuam vidēre? 27. Proximā nocte istōs virōs cōnvocāvistī. 28. Vītābimus istum furōrem ac tēla. 29. Fīnēs nostrī usque ad flūmen patent. 30. Jam diū hostium impetūs vītāre cōnāris. 31. Vigiliae urbis nocturnae mē nihil mōvērunt. 32. "Catilīna," Cicerō inquit, "cōnsilium contrā omnēs vītās nostrās jam diū capit." 33. Usque in senātum venit. 34. An nōs incendia nocturna ignōrāre arbitrāris? 35. Propter pestem pūblicam in oculīs cōnsulis furor erat.

Christian Prayers To Be Recited Daily, p. 214.—*The Sign of the Cross.* In the name of the Father and of the Son and of the Holy Spirit. Amen. *The Our Father.* Our Father, who art in heaven, *etc. The Hail Mary.* Hail, Mary, full of grace, *etc. The Doxology.* Glory be to the Father, and to the Son, *etc.*

Lesson 2

Exercise 4.—1. Cicero asks the senators what they think of the state. (*Sentiant,* Gr. 662.) 2. "What," he says, "do you think of the state?" 3. The senators did not know what they ought to think about the state. (*Debērent,* Gr. 662.) 4. Cicero asked what Catiline had done before dawn. (*Ēgisset,* Gr. 662.) 5. I shall ask who is waiting for me. (*Exspectet,* Gr. 662.) 6. We are not all unaware of where you were. (*Fuerīs,* Gr. 662.) 7. Do you know this? 8. I know what you will do. (*Factūrus sīs,* Gr. 530, 662; this is commonly known as the active periphrastic form.) 9. The eyes of many also see us while we are not noticing. 10. But the eyes of all the senators were turned upon Catiline. 11. Are you of consular rank or not? (*Annōn,* Gr. 505, 3.) 12. I asked whether you were of consular rank or not. (*Necne,* Gr. 661.) 13. Will you wait for me or not? (*Mēne,* Gr. 505, 2.) 14. I am altogether unaware of what those ancients decreed. (*Dēcrēverint,* Gr. 662.) 15. Cicero knew where Catiline had been, what he had done, whom he had called together, what plans he had made. (*Fuisset, ēgisset, convocāsset, cēpisset,* Gr. 662.) 16. I am not unaware how many men of consular rank there are in the Senate. (*Sint,* Gr. 662.) 17. Many did not understand what Christ was saying. (*Dīceret,* Gr. 662.) 18. I do not see how the voice of the people can be the voice of God. (*Possit,* Gr. 662.) 19. Are you willing to speak openly or will you remain silent? (*Utrum . . . an,* Gr. 505, 1.) 20. We were not all unaware of whether he wished to speak plainly or whether he would be silent. (*Vellet, tacēret,* Gr. 662.) 21. He asked me whether the voice of the consul was heard by all the senators. (*Audīrētur,* Gr. 662.) 22. I know why the consul's voice is not being heard by all who are in the Senate. (*Audiātur,* Gr. 662.) 23. Christ asked Peter whether he could watch one hour with Him. (*Posset,* Gr. 662.) 24. All men fear the punishments of the ancient laws. 25. Death is the supreme penalty of the state, is it not? 26. Cicero had a severe and weighty decree of the Senate against Catiline, according to which senatorial decree he should long since have been led to death. 27. Christ was led to death. 28. Cicero stated openly in the Senate that Catiline would be in arms on a certain day. 29. In the time of Catiline the Roman citizens were terrified by arms. 30. Catiline desired to destroy the world by murder and fire. 31. Many places of the city were marked down for fires. 32. Catiline was hemmed in on all sides; all his plans were clearer than the light of day. 33. The praetors were killed by the consul's hand. 34. But finally the praetor came to the place with a small band of soldiers. 35. The consul killed with his own hand a praetor who was eager for revolution. 36. War is an altogether destructive affair.

Exercise 5.—1. Ignōrāvit quot virī clārī in senātū essent. 2. Cicerō scīvit ubi Catilīna fuisset, quid ēgisset, quot virōs convocāsset. 3. Utrum mē audīvistī annōn? 4. Praetor rogāvit populum utrum eum audīvisset necne? 5. Cōnsul voluit scīre quid ūnusquisque dē hāc poenā gravī sentīret. 6. Cicerō nōn ignōrāvit ubi Catilīna esset. 7. Ex senātūs consultō ad mortem dūcī jam prīdem oportēbat. 8. Potesne audīre vōcem meam an clāra satis nōn est? 9. Nōn omnēs cīvēs vōcem praetōris audīre poterant nam nōn clāra erat. 10. Quid diceret Chrīstus multī nōn intellēxērunt. Oculōs habēbant at vidēre nōn poterant; mentēs habēbant at intellegere nōn poterant. 11. Pīlātus, dux Rōmānus, rogāvit Chrīstum utrum rex esset necne. 12. Chrīstus aperte dīxit sē regem esse at rēgnum suum ex hōc mundō nōn esse. 13. Illā nocte ipsā autem cīvis prīvātus cōnsulem occīdit. 14. Nōn dēcrēverat quam ad partem orbis terrārum sē itūrum esse. 15. Rogāvit aperte quō itūrus esset. 16. Dīxistī tē ex urbe īre dēcrēvisse. 17. Cōnsul cīvēs rogāvit quōmodo manūs mīlitum convocāvissent. 18. Jam prīdem hostēs perniciōsōs occīdere cupiēbant. 19. Quem populus Rōmānus timēbat? 20. Cicerō suōs rogāvit num Catilīna multōs hominēs perniciōsōs contrā rem pūblicam incitāret. 21. Nēmō scīvit ubi Catilīna esset. 22. Populus omnīnō ignōrāvit quantum periculum esset. 23. Rogāvit quōmodo cōnsiliī captī essent. 24. Nōnne Jūdas inimīcīs Chrīstum trādidit? 25. Temporibus antīquīs rēs pūblica ūnī virō saepe credita est propter timōrem rērum novārum. 26. Bella etiam antīqua perniciōsissima erant. 27. Praetor cōnsulārem prīvātus interfēcit. 28. Prīncipēs dēcrēvērunt perīculum prīvatum omnīnō vitāre.

Exercise 6.—Model: There was, there was once in this nation such manly courage that brave men would punish a dangerous citizen with harsher penalties than they would the bitterest foe.

1. Fuit, fuit ista quondam in Abraham virtūs ut fīlium ad mortem dūceret potius quam voluntātī Deī agendae dēficeret.

2. Fuit, fuit ista quondam in hāc rē pūblicā virtūs ut virī bonī ad mortem acriōrem cīvem quam magnum hostem dūcerent.

3. Fuit, fuit ista in hōc virō audācia ut orbem terrae tōtum incendiīs atque caede vastāret potius quam rem pūblicam dēfenderet.

Sight Translation, p. 220.—The Leaders of the Roman People. In the beginning the Roman people had kings. The first Roman king was Romulus. Romulus was a good king and fortified the city of Rome. All those who lived in the city had no fear. The Roman people praised Romulus. The Romans had in all seven kings.

Afterwards, however, the Roman people had consuls. There were two consuls, who were selected by the people. The power of a consul was

very great. At the time of Catiline's conspiracy one of the consuls was
Cicero. Cicero had seen that a conspiracy had been formed. He fortified
the place for holding the Senate. He summoned all the senators. He
entered the Senate. He overlooked nothing concerning the conspiracy.
All of Catiline's plans he disclosed.

Afterwards emperors ruled the Roman people. Of all the emperors
the greatest was Augustus Caesar. Since, however, not all the emperors
were good, the Roman state was overcome by barbarians.

Answer in Latin, p. 220.—1. By whom were the Romans ruled in
the beginning? (In prīncipiō populus Rōmānus rēgēs habuit.) 2. Who
was the first king of the Roman people? (Prīmus rēx erat Rōmulus.)
3. Romulus was good, wasn't he? (Ita, Rōmulus erat rēx bonus.)
4. What did Romulus do? (Rōmulus urbem Rōmam mūnīvit.) 5. Why
did the Romans praise him? (Populus Rōmānus Rōmulum laudāvit
quod erat rēx bonus.) 6. How many kings did the Romans have? (Rōmānī septem omnīnō habuērunt rēgēs.) 7. How many Roman consuls
were there? (Duo erant cōnsulēs.) 8. By whom were they chosen? (Ā
populō dēligēbantur.) 9. Was their power very great? (Imperium eōrum
erat maximum.) 10. Who was consul at the time of Catiline's conspiracy? (Tempore conjūrātiōnis Catilīnae cōnsul erat Cicerō.) 11. What
did Cicero do? (Cicerō vīdit conjūrātiōnem esse factam et, senātōribus
convōcātīs, omnia cōnsilia patēfēcit.) 12. Who ruled the Roman people
afterwards? (Posteā imperātōrēs populum Rōmānum regēbant.)
13. Who was the greatest emperor of all? (Omnium imperātōrum maximus erat Augustus Caesar.) 14. All the Roman emperors were not
good, were they? (Nōn omnēs imperātōrēs erant bonī.)

Lesson 3

Exercise 7.—1. May good times come. (*Veniant*, Gr. 511.) 2. May
Christ's kingdom come. (*Veniat*, Gr. 511.) 3. May we be good to the
end of our lives. (*Sīmus*, Gr. 511.) 4. May they not lead the brave man
to death. (*Dūcant*, Gr. 511.) 5. Thy kingdom come. (*Adveniat*, Gr.
511.) 6. May Christ conquer, may Christ rule, may Christ command!
(*Vincat, rēgnet, imperet*, Gr. 511.) 7. Would that Caesar had escaped
death. (*Vītāsset*, Gr. 513.) 8. Would that Cicero were living. (*Vīveret*,
Gr. 512.) 9. Would that Judas had not betrayed Christ. (*Trādidisset*,
Gr. 513.) 10. May we find the way. (*Inveniāmus*, Gr. 511.) 11. May the
will of God be done by all, in every place, at every moment. (*Fīat*, Gr.
511.) 12. May the world not be destroyed by the wickedness of men.
(*Vastētur*, Gr. 511.) 13. May good times come in our state. (*Veniant*,

Gr. 511.) 14. Would that the soldiers had held the walls. (*Tenuissent*, Gr. 513.) 15. Long live the consul! Long live our city! Long live our state! Long live our people! Long live our laws! (*Vīvat, vīvant*, Gr. 511.) 16. Would that all men would strive after a good character. (*Studērent*, Gr. 512.) 17. Would that the Jews had not led Christ to death. (*Dūxissent*, Gr. 513.) 18. May we all after death come to God. (*Veniāmus*, Gr. 511.) 19. May you live many years. (*Vīvās*, Gr. 511.) 20. Would that all wicked and desperate men were putting away wickedness and keeping the laws of the state. (*Dēpōnerent, servārent*, Gr. 512.) 21. Cicero saw a band of wicked men daily plotting the ruin of the state. 22. May the number of cruel wars not increase. (*Crēscat*, Gr. 511.) 23. For a certain reason the praetor had not yet seized the wicked man. 24. Good times have not yet come. 25. Depraved men plot revolution within the state rather than foreign wars. 26. As yet we have not a senatorial decree of this kind. 27. Would that all men had understood what the rights of a private citizen were. (*Comprehendissent*, Gr. 513.) 28. May we all grow in virtue day by day. (*Crēscāmus*, Gr. 511.) 29. May he rather put down recklessness than encourage it. (*Dēpōnat, cōnfirmet*, Gr. 511.) 30. Praetors who do all things justly cannot yet be found. 31. The ancients had long been thinking that they could kill a man who was eager for revolution. 32. Publius Scipio killed Tiberius Gracchus without official authority. 33. Death cannot be avoided.

Exercise 8.—1. Utinam rēgnum Chrīstī veniat. 2. Nē omnēs improbī perditīque cīvēs ad reī pūblicae perniciem vītās suās dēpōnerent. 3. Utinam perniciēs eō tempore nē vēnisset. 4. Nē veniat. 5. Vīvat Chrīstus Rēx! 6. Utinam hominēs crūdēlēs nē essent. 7. Tempora bona veniant. 8. Hostēs ad mūrōs urbis nōndum vēnērunt. 9. Utinam jūra cīvium ā senātū comprehenderentur. 10. Utinam timor populī Catilīnam mōvisset. 11. Utinam omnēs hominēs rēgnum Chrīstī cuperent. 12. Utinam patientiam habeāmus. 13. Ad multōs annōs vīvās. 14. Utinam perniciem ējus modī in rē pūblicā vītēmus. 15. Laudētur Jēsus Chrīstus! 16. Nē moenia antīqua inveniat. 17. Utinam urbēs Eurōpae bellō nē vastātae essent. 18. Utinam omnēs Chrīstiānī voluntātī Deī studērent. 19. Dux conjūrātiōnis improbus potius quam crūdēlis erat. 20. Nē cīvēs ējus modī intrā mūrōs urbis nostrae inveniantur. 21. Virtūs ējus crēscat. 22. Utinam manus hominum perditōrum propter nēquitiam suam comprehēnsa esset. 23. Mīlitēs improbī caedem cīvium nōn dēpōnēbant. 24. Nōs vīcēsimum jam diem tē exspectāmus. 25. Populus Rōmānus jam prīdem rēbus novīs studēbant. 26. Brutus manū suā Caesarem occīdit. 27. Perniciem urbis jam prīdem mōliēbātur. 28. Nōs vīcēsimum jam diem cōnsulem in senātū nōn invenimus. 29. Conjūrātiō propter nēquitiam cōnsulis crēscēbat.

Exercise 9.—Model: Then at last you will be put to death when no one can any longer be found so depraved, so abandoned, so like yourself as not to admit that the deed has been done in full justice.

1. Tum dēnique omnēs hominēs beātī erunt cum jam nēmō tam improbus, tam perditus, invenīrī poterit quī Deum nōn dīligat.

2. Tum dēnique hostēs vincēmus cum jam nēmō tam ignāvus, tam perditus, invenīrī poterit quī prō rē pūblicā nōn pugnet.

3. Tum dēnique mundus tōtus pācem habēbit cum jam nēmō tam stultus, tam improbus, invenīrī poterit quī jūra omnium gentium nōn servet.

Exercise 10 [Amans Patriae Tyrannum Adloquitur].—Jam diū urbem nostram vastāre cupis. Jam diū rēbus novīs studēs. Nihilne timōre populī movēris? Nōnne vidēs omnēs bonōs in hāc urbe omnia scīre? Nōnne vidēs cōnsilia tua ab omnī populō scīrī? Quem nostrum in hāc rē pūblicā arbitrāris ignōrāre quid proximā aut superiōre nocte ēgerīs? Tōta orbis terrārum scīvit tē locum mūnītum habēre quō manus tua sē recipit.

Omnēs hominēs bonī quid cōnsilī capiant. Utinam ēgissēmus. Omnia vidēmus et intellegimus; nihil agimus. Tempus veniat cum eī quī rēbus novīs studeant ad mortem dūcantur.

Lesson 4

Exercise 11.—1. "I have come," he said, "and I am here in the Senate." (*Vēnī*, Gr. 493.) 2. Cicero had fortified with great care the place for holding Senate. (*Mūnīverat*, Gr. 494.) 3. All good citizens strive after courage. (*Student*, Gr. 484.) 4. The influence of this state is good in every place. (*Est*, Gr. 483.) 5. Cicero not only heard but also saw everything that Catiline had done. (*Fēcerat*, Gr. 495.) 6. One consul was living in the state; the other had for a long time been in the province. (*Vīvēbat*, Gr. 486; *fuerat*, Gr. 495.) 7. All men suffer death. (*Patiuntur*, Gr. 484.) 8. Cicero comes into the Senate, he summons everyone, he discloses all. (*Venit, convocat, patefacit*, Gr. 485.) 9. There was once in the Roman state great manly courage. (*Fuit*, Gr. 492.) 10. The consul dared to lead the enemy to death. (*Audēbat*, Gr. 486.) 11. We shall burst forth from the fortified city. (*Ērumpēmus*, Gr. 489.) 12. All who had heard Christ wondered. (*Audīverant*, Gr. 495.) 13. Christ did all that His Father had said. (*Dīxerat*, Gr. 495.) 14. Then men were suffering death on account of virtue. (*Patiēbantur*, Gr. 486.)

15. All the citizens were guarding their homes with extraordinary care. (*Custōdiēbant*, Gr. 486.) 16. The eye is the light of the mind. (*Est*, Gr. 484.) 17. Neither the darkness of night can hide nor a private home restrain within its walls your impious meetings. (*Potest*, Gr. 483.) 18. Catiline with his wicked followers was striving after revolution. (*Studēbat*, Gr. 486.) 19. Finally a fierce war comes. (*Venit*, Gr. 485.) 20. They were much more surprised at the consul's care than at the praetor's recklessness. (*Admīrābantur*, Gr. 486.) 21. Men often change their minds. (*Mūtant*, Gr. 484.) 22. Cicero did not yet dare to do what he ought to have done. (*Audēbat, dēbēbat*, Gr. 486.) 23. The citizens burst forth from the Senate. (*Ērumpunt*, Gr. 483 or 485.) 24. They are also fleeing from the towns. (*Profugiunt*, Gr. 483.) 25. No one was able to restrain the assemblage. (*Potuit*, Gr. 492.) 26. We all forget many things, even those we should remember. (*Oblīvīscimur*, Gr. 484; *oportet*, Gr. 483.) 27. Wicked citizens are much more alert for the ruin of the state than the good are for its welfare. (*Vigilant*, Gr. 484.) 28. Gentlemen of the Senate, we must act now, now! (*Oportet*, Gr. 483.) 29. But for a very good reason we have not yet been induced to do what ought to have been done long ago. (*Oportuit*, Gr. 492; *addūcimur*, Gr. 483.) 30. The consul came into camp before dawn. (*Vēnit*, Gr. 492.) 31. Cicero had come into the Senate long before. (*Vēnerat*, Gr. 494.) 32. He asked me what I had waited for. (*Exspectāvissem*, Gr. 495, 531.) 33. The leader was waiting for the darkness of night. (*Exspectābat*, Gr. 486.) 34. Cicero had long been awaiting the authority of the Senate. (*Exspectābat*, Text pp. 210-211.) 35. Catiline, leader of the enemy and chief of the conspiracy, was expected daily by his men. (*Exspectābātur*, Gr. 486.) 36. No one dares now to defend Catiline. (*Audet*, Gr. 483 or 485.) 37. We, however, do not dare to do what our forefathers did. (*Audēmus*, Gr. 483.) 38. The enemy of the state comes within the walls, and now even into the Senate. (*Venit*, Gr. 483.) 39. Good citizens and enemies of the state are now held within the same walls. (*Continentur*, Gr. 483 or 485.) 40. The consul has long been restrained by the armed forces of the enemy. (*Continētur*, Text pp. 210-211.) 41. Peter remembered the words of Christ and on that night was moved even to tears. (*Meminerat*, Gr. 437.) 42. Christ has never forgotten sinners. (*Est oblītus*, Gr. 493.) 43. Do you remember everything that Cicero said in the Senate, or have you forgotten much? (*Es oblītus*, Gr. 493.)

Exercise 12.—1. Tempōribus antīquīs cōnsulēs multō facilius ad mortem hominēs ducēbant. 2. Cicerō Catilīnae furōrem ac tēla diū vītābat. 3. Chrīstus nihil agēbat nisi quod Pater eī dīxerat. 4. Nullus Chrīstiānus ignōrat Deum esse unum. 5. Numerus coetuum nefāriōrum in hāc urbe incredibilis est. 6. Jam diū nōn modo urbem sed etiam domōs et vītās contrā hominum improbōrum impetūs atrōcēs dēfendimus. 7. Antīquīs tempōribus populus Rōmānus magnam auctōritātem habuerat; senātus autem ā manibus eōrum eam cēpit. 8. Cicerō vērum conjūrātiōnem dīligentiā incredibile repressit. Ille cōnsul nōn modo omnia vidēbat sed etiam dē coetibus nefāriīs audiēbat. 9. Nōs omnēs mortem patiēmur. 10. Auctōritās unīus virī bonī multōs ad virtūtem commovēre potest. 11. Senātūs consultum grave fuerat. 12. Ex ējus modī senātūs consultō omnēs virī quī in urbem cum tēlīs venīre ausī erant interfectī erant. 13. Cicerō usque ad timōrem nōn commōtus est, nam nōn talis erat. 14. Omnēs ea quae Chrīstus dicēbat admirātī sunt. Verba ējus in mente magnā dīligentiā servāvērunt. 15. Mīlitēs ex castrīs fūgerant et nemō impedimenta servāre ausus est. 16. Chrīstiānī sciunt omnem auctōritātem ā Deō venīre. 17. Omnēs cīvēs vivent, dux eōrum autem ad mortem ducētur. 18. Deus Pater omnium hominum est. 19. Noctēs et diēs propter conjūrātiōnem atrōcem in timōre vivēbat. 20. Cum patre vēnit. 21. Manus cīvium domō fūgērunt. 22. Omnis auctōritās in manū Chrīstī est, nam Deus est. 23. Omnēs Chrīstiānī bonī fierī similēs Chrīstī student. 24. Catilīna nihil dixit; oblītus erat omnia quae in cōnsiliō dicere voluerat. 25. Estne patientia virtūs Chrīstiāna? 26. Omnēs oblīvīscimur multa quae meminisse nōs oportet. 27. Rōmānī urbēs suās nōn modō custōdiēbant sed etiam moenibus mūniēbant. 28. Deus omnia quae fecerat vīdit et bona erant. 29. Petrus meminerat quae Chrīstus dīxerat. 30. Hostis atrōx ex castrīs incredibile furōre ērūpit. 31. Mentem nōn mūtāvit sed ex urbe ad castra ērūpit. 32. Multō magis admirātī sunt dīligentiam incredibilem quā domum custōdiēbant. 33. Multōs jam diēs castra hostium in Italiā sunt. 34. Chrīstiānī jam diū intelligunt oportuisse Chrīstum ad mortem ducī.

Exercise 13.—Omnia cōnsilia tua nōbīs clarissima sunt. Ubi superiōre nocte fuerīs, quōs ex urbe emīserīs, quōs hominēs improbōs convocāverīs—omnēs scīmus atque intelligimus. Continēris undique ā custōdibus reī pūblicae. Commovēre tē contrā urbem, cōnsulēs, rem pūblicam nōn potes. Nōnne haec sentīs? Nōnne vidēs nōs omnia scīre? Jam prīdem oportēbat tē tua cōnsilia mūtāre et caedem cīvium perniciemque reī pūblicae oblīvīscī.

From the Roman Missal, p. 233.—From the Ordinary of the Mass. Glory be to God in the highest, and on earth peace to men of good will. We praise Thee. We bless Thee. We adore Thee. We glorify Thee.

We give Thee thanks for Thy great glory, O Lord God, heavenly King, God the Father almighty. O Lord, the only-begotten Son, Jesus Christ; O Lord God, Lamb of God, Son of the Father, who takest away the sins of the world, have mercy on us. Thou who takest away the sins of the world, receive our prayer. Thou who sittest at the right hand of the Father, have mercy on us. For Thou alone art holy, Thou alone art Lord, Thou alone, O Jesus Christ, art most high, together with the Holy Spirit in the glory of God the Father. Amen.

From the Proper of the Saints. Let us pray. O God, whose only-begotten Son through His life, death, and resurrection has prepared for us the eternal rewards of salvation: grant, we beseech Thee, that commemorating these mysteries by means of the most sacred rosary of blessed Mary, we may imitate what they contain and may attain what they promise. Through the same Jesus Christ Thy Son, our Lord, who liveth and reigneth with Thee in the unity of the Holy Spirit, forever and ever. Amen.

Lesson 5

Exercise 14.—1. We are all in this place. (*Hōc*, Gr. 794.) 2. Our fathers are in that place. (*Eō*, Gr. 794.) 3. Cicero was in that place. (*Illō*, Gr. 794.) 4. That madness of yours does not move us. (*Iste*, Gr. 799.) 5. Cicero and Catiline were Romans; the latter formed the conspiracy; the former exposed the conspiracy. (*Hic, ille*, Gr. 795.) 6. We will fortify this city; we will not strengthen that one. (*Hanc, illam*, Gr. 795.) 7. He said all those things in the Senate. (*Illa*, Gr. 793.) 8. Those who are depraved and desperate cannot be good citizens. (*Ii*, Gr. 797.) 9. The famous Cicero was the leader of the Roman people. (*Ille*, Gr. 798.) 10. Brutus killed with his own hand the famous Caesar. (*Illum*, Gr. 798.) 11. That fellow Catiline was contemplating the ruin of his own city and even of the whole world. (*Iste*, Gr. 799.) 12. Shall we pass over in silence this extraordinary crime? (*Hōc*, Gr. 794.) 13. You can in no manner make a move against the state. (*Tē*, Gr. 800.) 14. In the time of Cicero desperate men could not make a move against a fortified city. (*Sē*, Gr. 803.) 15. Would that we could all see ourselves as others see us. (*Nōs*, Gr. 800.) 16. Several citizens had betaken themselves to the same city. (*Sē*, Gr. 803.) 17. Plainly, no one can give to others what he himself does not have. (*Ipse*, Gr. 808.) 18. Cicero praised himself to the very end. (*Sē*, Gr. 803.) 19. May we not be eulogizers of our own time. (*Nostrī*, Gr. 800.) 20. Would that the immortal gods were giving you that mind! (*Istam*, Gr. 792.)

21. Caesar said his men were coming. (*Suōs*, Gr. 802.) 22. Catiline had long since felt sure that he would take the city in a night attack. (*Sē*, Gr. 803.) 23. Catiline ordered all his men to come with him. (*Sēcum*, Gr. 803.) 24. Christ Himself was led to death with two wicked men, but one of them was moved by the patience of Christ. Christ strengthened his courage. "Today," He said, "you will be with Me in heaven." And he who was once wicked and abandoned, in the hour of death is numbered among the saints. (*Ipse*, Gr. 808; *illīs*, Gr. 806; *ējus*, Gr. 806; *mēcum*, Gr. 800; *ille*, Gr. 797.) 25. Christ came unto His own, and His own killed Him. (*Suōs, suī*, Gr. 802.) 26. Virtue is good in itself. (*Ipsa*, Gr. 808.) 27. The consul was not yet wounding with so much as a word the enemies of the state. 28. Cicero praised himself to the end. (*Ipse*, Gr. 810.) 29. They were thinking daily of our own ruin. (*Ipsōrum*, Gr. 811.) 30. You will see your own father, won't you? (*Ipsīus*, Gr. 811.) 31. He himself spoke. (*Ipse*, Gr. 812.) 32. Catiline called together a band of men. He himself, their leader, came to them on that night. (*Ipse*, Gr. 812; *eōrum*, Gr. 806.) 33. Cicero strengthened the night garrison, and himself came into the Senate with a weapon. (*Ipse*, Gr. 812.) 34. We can all be strengthened by knowledge of the saints themselves. (*Ipsōrum*, Gr. 808.) 35. But I myself plainly saw the city's ruin at that time. (*Ipse*, Gr. 808.) 36. They destroyed the same place by fire. They had killed the good citizens with their own hands. (*Ipsī*, Gr. 812; *suā*, Gr. 802.) 37. Why are you silent? 38. In our times a private citizen cannot kill a public enemy on his own authority. (*Suā*, Gr. 802.) 39. Those ancient Romans of whom Cicero spoke did this very thing. (*Illī*, Gr. 797; *ipsum*, Gr. 809.) 40. The commander led his troops into camp. He himself moved against the enemy. (*Suōs*, Gr. 802; *ipse*, Gr. 812; *sē*, Gr. 803.) 41. When I come I myself will see you. (*Ipse*, Gr. 808.) 42. May God be with you daily. (*Vōbīscum*, Gr. 124, note 1.) 43. No one had seen a man of such recklessness. For that fellow desired nothing except the ruin of the state. (*Iste*, Gr. 799.) 44. For a good reason his father ordered him to come to him. (*Ējus, eum*, Gr. 806; *sē*, Gr. 803.) 45. Nor have I seen anywhere a man so wicked, so abandoned, so like Catiline. 46. The camp was pitched in Italy itself. The leader himself had come into the Senate. (*Ipsā, ipse*, Gr. 808.) 47. May God strengthen us daily against all dangers from the enemy. 48. But you see their leader in the Senate. (*Eōrum*, Gr. 806.) 49. You have affirmed that you yourself will go out directly. (*Ipsum*, Gr. 808.)

Exercise 15.—1. Sunt quī ducēs suōs nōn dīligant. 2. Hīc sunt in nostrō numerō quī reī pūblicae exitium ipsum plānē cupiant. 3. Audācia istīus hominis mē nihil movet. 4. Quae erat hūjus sceleris causa? 5. Ego ipse plānē ignōrō. 6. Dux dīxit castra sua in Italiā posita esse. 7. Cicerō ipse idem dīxit. 8. Complūrēs proeliō illō vulnerātī sunt. 9. Hic cīvis bonus est, ille autem improbus. 10. Erant quī dūcere Chrīstum ad mortem studēbant (studērent, *if treated as a characteristic clause*). 11. Dux ille Caesar contrā senātūs auctōritātem suōs Rōmam dūxit. 12. Plānē nullus homō immortalis est. 13. Utinam dē scelere tacuissēmus. 14. Cōnfīdere tantō hostium numerō nōn possumus. 15. Imperātor ipse nullam ratiōnem certam habēbat. 16. Eōdem locō mīlitēs complūrēs cotīdiē vulnerantur. 17. Sunt quī Deum nōn vereantur. 18. Utinam nōs omnēs mortem aeternam vītēmus. 19. Certā dē causā Cicerō locum ipsum habendī senātus ṃūnīvit. 20. Utinam Italia ducem perditum nōn habuisset; illa autem ad exitium ā virō unō ducta est. 21. Cum veneris, ipse tē vidēbō. 22. Virtūs est bona in sē. 23. Multa scelera cōtidiē cogitābat, sed dē eīs nihil agēbat. 24. Complūrēs Rōmānī sē dīs immortālibus cōnfīdere posse crēdidērunt.

Exercise 16 [Ōratiō Amantis Patriae Cīvibus].—Hīc, hīc sunt in nostrō numerō, cīvēs, quī contrā cīvitātem, rem pūblicam, populum nostrum conjūrātiōnem faciant. In diēs numerus eōrum quī rērum novārum cupidī sunt crēscit. Hīc, hīc est in cīvitāte nostrā castra contrā nōs omnēs mūnīta. Dūcem istīus manūs hominum improbōrum et perditōrum in urbe et etiam in senātū vidētis. Nōs vērō, populī dūcēs, quid agimus? Hīc unum locum mūnīmus, ibi alterum. Furōrem ac tela hūjus imperatōris perditī vītāmus et nōs omnia agere arbitrāmur.

Nōnne ad mortem dūcī jam prīdem oportēbat? Patrēs nōstrī nōn erant hūjus modī hominēs. Cum ipsī vīdērunt conjūrātiōnem factam esse manibus suīs improbōs occīdērunt. Urbem mūnīvērunt. Contrā perīculum omnēs cīvēs bonōs cōnfirmāvērunt.

Utinam hīs tempōribus nostrīs virōs talēs habērēmus. Utinam nōs, populī dūcēs, virtūtem patrum nostrōrum habērēmus. Nōs vērō iam diū istum virum ac omnem ējus manum improbōrum in audāciā immō furōre sē cōnfirmāre patimur. Rēs tōta, cīvēs, gravis est. Hoc est tempus agendī. Furōrem ac tēla hostium vītāre diūtius nōn possumus. Deus prō nōbīs est, quī cum prō nōbīs est, quis contrā nōs esse potest?

Lesson 6

Exercise 17.—1. We, however, brave citizens that we are, praise the consul if he avoids the mad weapons of that fellow. (*Laudāmus, vītat,* Gr. 581.) 2. If I order you killed, will it please the Roman people? (*Jusserō,* Gr. 581.) 3. But if I order you to be seized, no one will be so wicked and so depraved as to miss you. (*Sin autem*, Gr. 587.) 4. The praetors wanted to lead out with him all Catiline's friends, but if not all, as many as possible. (*Sī minus*, Gr. 588.) 5. If my fellow citizens feared me, I should at last leave the city. (*Timerent*, Gr. 583.) 6. If you deny it, I will prove your guilt! (*Negās*, Gr. 581.) 7. If I had said this in the Senate, it would not have pleased the consuls. (*Dīxissem, placuisset*, Gr. 583.) 8. If I should speak of these matters with you, what would you think? (*Loquar, cōgitēs*, Gr. 582.) 9. Unless Cicero had determined to lead Catiline to death, Rome would not have been freed from fear. (*Statuisset, esset līberāta*, Gr. 583, 584.) 10. If I were king, I would choose my friends with great care. (*Essem*, Gr. 583.) 11. If I were in camp, I should miss my home. (*Essem, dēsīderārem*, Gr. 583.) 12. If a crime is not private but public, it ought to be checked by sharper punishments. (*Sī nōn*, Gr. 585.) 13. But if I declare these things, you will plainly deny them. (*Praedīxerō, negābis*, Gr. 581.) 14. If the praetors had come a little before dawn, they would have discovered everything. (*Vēnissent, comperissent*, Gr. 583.) 15. If at that time Catiline had gone out to the Manlian camp, this would now be pleasing to all the citizens. (*Ēgressus esset, placēret*, Gr. 593.) 16. If at some time it pleases you to remain in this city for a little while, you can stay with me. (*Poteris*, Gr. 581.)

Exercise 18.—1. Sī Catilīnae placēret ex urbe exīre, metū cīvitātem līberāret. 2. Sī Cicerō hoc nōn praedīxisset, populus id nōn comperisset. 3. Nisi Catilīna in senātum paulō ante vēnisset, Cicerō haec nōn dīxisset. 4. Sī Catilīna aliquandō ex urbe egrederētur, manēretne Cicerō? 5. Nisi Cicerō populum timuisset, Catilīnam ad mortem dūcere statuisset. 6. Sī aliquandō ex urbe egrederis, metū mē līberābis. 7. Sīn autem tibi placet, dēlige complūrēs virēs fortēs. 8. Senātuī praedīxī tē interficere mē statuisse. 9. Sī in urbe nōn vīverēs, domum tuam dēsīderārēs. 10. Sī praetōrēs in domum ējus paulō ante noctem ductī essent, coetum nēfarium comperissent. 11. Quodsī domō abessēmus, amīcōs nostrōs paulum dēsīderārēmus. 12. Sī custōdēs ad portās posuerō, nēmō in urbem venīre poterit. 13. Sī mīlitēs quōs in ponte statuerat fortēs fuissent, hostēs reppulissent.

Exercise 19.—1. Sī Catilīnam jam diū timēmus, cur eum interficī nōn jubēmus? 2. Sī in senātum venīre iste vir perditus audēret, eum ēdūcerēmus. 3. Sī certam causam habuisset, nōbīs plānē praedīxisset. 4. Sī rem pūblicam dīligentiā dēfendere nōn potuimus, eam gladiō dēfendere nōn poterimus. 5. Nisi Cicerō locum habendī senātum mūnīvisset, Catilīna suīque eum cēpissent. 6. Sī Deus bonus est, cur nōn omnēs hominēs eum dīligunt? 7. Nisi Chrīstus Deus esset, summam laudem eī nōn darēmus. 8. Sī Catilīna Cicerōnem interfēcisset, Rōma vastāta esset. 9. Cīvitās firma esse nōn potest nisi cīvēs ducēs bonōs dēligunt. 10. Sī audāciam vītāveris, in scientiā crēscēs. 11. Ipsam urbem nostrōrum nōn mūnīvimus. 12. Nēmō Deum intellegere potest sicut Deus sē ipsum intellegit. 13. Sīn autem paulō ante mediam noctem venerēs, mē domī inveniās. 14. Sī frāter vīveret, eum nōn dēsīderārem.

Exercise 20.—Model: You said that some little delay was occasioned to you by the fact that I was yet alive (You said that you even now hesitated a little because I was still living).

1. Dīxistī tē in perīculō gravī esse quod ego vēnissem.

2. Dīxistī tē etiam tum paulō longius mansisse quod cōnsul dīligentior esset tē ipsō.

3. Dīxit aliquantum sibi esse etiam nunc timōris quod cōnsul cōnsilia sua scīret.

Exercise 21 [Patriae Amans Cīvēs Defectiōnis Americanae Congregātōs Appellat].—Hīc in ipsō nostrō numerō, in hōc gravī conventū colōniārum, sunt quī dē interitū colōniārum nostrārum ac nostrum omnium cogitent. Sunt quī statuerint nōs hostibus trādere, pacem contrā nostram voluntātem cum Britannīs facere, dēnique lībertātem trādere quam ā majōribus nostrīs accēpimus quamque ut conservēmus nunc pugnāmus.

Exercise 22.—1. Quō īs? 2. Pugnābō usque ad fīnem. 3. Impetūs jam diū contrā nōs omnēs facis. 4. Nōnne istam pestem reī pūblicae ad mortem dūcēmus? 5. Placuit senātuī Catilīnam ad mortem dūcī. 6. An arbitrāris Catilīnam bonum esse? 7. Scīsne quam diū Chrīstus in terrā fuerit? 8. Quid nunc suscipis? 9. Cōnsulem ipsum eum occīdere oportet. 10. Washingtonius cīvitātem ab hostibus dēfendit. 11. Nēmō tam improbus invenīrī potuit, quī Washingtonium nōn laudāret. 12. Nēmō est quī ignōret Washingtonium fortem fuisse. 13. Washingtonius Pater Patriae appellātus est. 14. Britannī oppida colōniārum urbēsque vastābant. 15. Washingtonius dīligentiā sua et auxiliō omnium hominum bonōrum eōs reppulit. 16. Rēs pūblica nostra ab eō nōn modō servāta sed etiam līberāta est. 17. Maximās grātiās Deō debēmus quod hunc virum nōbīs dedit. 18. Oportet omnēs Americānōs Washingtonium ob oculōs semper habēre.

Exercise 23.—Model: You can dwell among us no longer. I will not bear it, I will not suffer it, I will not permit it.

1. In urbe manēre jam diūtius nōn potest, cōnsul nōn sinet, senātus nōn patiētur, dī immortālēs nōn ferent.

2. Īnsidiās istās nōn ignōrāmus, omnia audīmus, omnia cognoscimus, omnia intellegimus.

3. Contrā cīvēs pugnāre jam diūtius nōn potes, nōn feram, nōn patiar.

4. Cōnsilium tuum inīre nunc potes, cōnsul nihil faciet, insidiās neque audiet neque vidēbit.

5. In rem pūblicam bellum gerere jam diūtius nōn potes, neque amīcī neque hostēs tuī sinent, dī immortālēs ipsī nōn patientur.

Lesson 7

Exercise 24.—1. Let them not contemplate this disaster. (*Nē cōgitent*, Gr. 514.) 2. Be silent, all! (*Tacēte*, Gr. 515.) 3. Do not seize the temple. (*Nōlīte occupāre*, Gr. 516.) 4. Don't deny that you are my ally. (*Nē negāverīs*, Gr. 516.) 5. Let us hear what the speaker says. (*Audiāmus*, Gr. 518.) 6. Let us not think evil thoughts about our allies. (*Nē cōgitēmus*, Gr. 518.) 7. Let our allies preserve Rome. (*Cōnservent*, Gr. 514.) 8. Check the enemy's attack, soldiers. (*Reprimite*, Gr. 515.) 9. "Remember me, Lord, when you come into Your kingdom." (*Mementō*, Gr. 515.) 10. Be brave in your exile. (*Estōte*, Gr. 515.) 11. Show us, O Lord, the way of salvation. (*Ostende*, Gr. 515.) 12. Change that attitude of yours now. (*Mūtā*, Gr. 515.) 13. Forget slaughter and conflagrations. (*Oblīvīscere*, Gr. 515.) 14. Let them leave the city with all their companions. (*Exeant*, Gr. 514.) 15. Finally, recall with me that night before last. (*Recognōsce*, Gr. 515.) 16. Remember, man, your last end. (*Mementō*, Gr. 515.) 17. Don't hesitate longer. (*Nōlī dubitāre*, Gr. 516.) 18. Don't say that. (*Nē dīxerīs*, Gr. 516.) 19. By Thy paths, O Lord, lead us on our way to eternal salvation. (*Dūc*, Gr. 515.) 20. Wars overwhelm us, Lord; give us strength, bring us help. (*Dā, fer*, Gr. 515.) 21. Come, my son, and help me. (*Venī, adjuvā*, Gr. 515.) 22. Let us make for the buildings of the city. (*Petāmus*, Gr. 518.) 23. Come, Holy Spirit, enlighten us. (*Venī, dā*, Gr. 515.) 24. Hear, O Lord, my prayer and let my cry come unto You. (*Audī*, Gr. 515; *veniat*, Gr. 514.) 25. From every evil deliver us, O Lord. (*Līberā*, Gr. 515.) 26. St. Peter, pray for us. (*Ōrā*, Gr. 515.) 27. Let us pray both for our friends and for our enemies. (*Ōrēmus*, Gr. 518.) 28. Come, let us praise the Lord. (*Venīte*, Gr. 515.) 29. Let us see, friends, what is in this city. (*Videāmus*, Gr. 518.) 30. Hold firmly those good friends you have. (*Tenēte*, Gr. 515.) 31. Of his own will the leader sought death rather than exile. 32. I hate the uproar of assemblies. 33. A certain soldier wanted to kill Cicero at the last consular elections. 34. Although exile is evil, there are some who do not hesitate to accept this penalty for the sake of the state. 35. Catiline was pondering not exile but a threatening war. 36. They fortified the whole temple. 37. Wherefore all men fear the harshness of exile and seek to escape this misfortune. 38. Wait for me outside the walls of the city. 39. Although the consul both hated and feared the enemy, he did not wish to send him into exile. 40. Certain enemies were daily plotting against the citizens. 41. "How long," said Cicero, "have you been plotting against me, the consul-elect!" 42. If my friends should fear and hate me, I would withdraw from their sight.

Exercise 25.—1. On that night several companions of your criminal madness had come to the house of Marcus Laecus. 2. I have not only heard of his sternness, but I have even seen it. 3. Hear, good servant, the voice of your master. 4. Cicero did not merely perceive Catiline's plans, but also checked them. 5. Let us all be silent within these walls. 6. Why should we be silent? 7. The soldiers seized the city in a night attack, for it had not been fortified. 8. You do not dare to deny this, do you? 9. Certain leading men of the state fled from Rome at the time when Catiline marked them for assassination. 10. May our souls be preserved from sin. 11. The son did nothing, thought nothing that his father did not only hear but also see and clearly perceive. 12. Catiline's companions were discussing certain things among themselves. 13. Christ was crucified between two criminals. 14. I likewise said this. 15. For Cicero had seen in the Senate certain men who were associated with Catiline. 16. The state was once freed from fear for a short space of time by the carefulness of the consul. 17. Cicero said likewise that he had fortified that same place. 18. The soldiers finally arrived at the temple. 19. They made an attack against the houses. 20. Catiline's companions were discussing among themselves every crime. 21. Heart of Jesus, say to us, "I am your salvation." 22. Christ is the prince of peace. 23. In this state we have no fortified city. 24. Why did the consul not hesitate to ask for exile of his own accord? 25. Lead out all your men with you; clean out the city.

Exercise 26.—1. Cōgitā bene, puer, dē hīs. 2. Nōn modō taceāmus sed etiam tumultum vītēmus. 3. Nē negāverīs tē in domō Laecae (apud Laecam) fuisse. 4. Occupāte oppidum, mīlitēs, tecta autem cīvium cōnservāte. 5. Dūc nōs, Domine, ad regnum tuum. 6. Bonum agite, malum vītāte. 7. Līberent cōnsulēs rem pūblicam ā perniciē. 8. Mūtā istam mentem, fīlī mī. 9. Semper parātī sīmus. 10. Nē dubitāveritis, patrēs cōnscrīptī, dē hāc perniciē mentem mūtāre. 11. Quārē nōlīte metuere sevēritātem ējus. 12. Ego īdem dīxī mē eī comitiīs consulāribus īnsidiātūrum esse. 13. Oblīvīscere incendiōrum atque gladiōrum (caedium). 14. Nē neget sē in comitūs fuisse. 15. Nē īnsidientur praetōrī domī ējus. 16. Vītēmus hoc bellum infestum. 17. Cicerō īdem dīxit sociōs sceleris suī sub idem tēctum convēnisse. 18. Fugant prīncipēs a Rōmā. 19. Nē negāverīs tē haec dixisse. 20. Mūniant mīlitēs nōn modō senātum sed etiam prīncipum tecta. 21. Ego īdem dīxī sē suā sponte ad castra extrā moenia itūrum esse. 22. Propter unum hominem quidam tumultus in urbe erat. 23. Ōrēmus nōn modō prō amīcīs vērum etiam prō inimīcīs nostrīs. 24. Quaerāmus cūr in exilium mittantur. 25. Dux aliquandō tacuit. Diū locūtus erat, immō nimium diū. 26. Huic hominī nē crēdideris. 27. Nē īnsidiētur reī pūblicae. 28. Exeat ūnā cum omnibus suīs. 29. Nē sit ullus tumultus in hōc sānctissimō templō. 30. Quamquam calamitās infestissima erat, quidam virī nōn dubitāvērunt eī resistere. 31. Nōlīte crēdere rem pūblicam cīvibus perniciōsīs. 32. Inveniāmus viam. 33. Lībertātem nostram maximā dīligentiā custōdiāmus.

Exercise 27.—Mūtāte istam mentem, cīvēs; salūtem vestram cōnservāre diūtius nōn potestis. Īte, mūnīte domōs, parāte vōs contrā hostēs. In Italiā contrā vōs castra posita sunt. Hostēs impetum facient quō tempore nōn exspectētis. Cōnfirmāte virtūtem vestram, dēfendite domōs, custōdīte populum. Undique continēmur. Oportet nōs omnēs pugnāre ut lībertātem nostram servēmus.

Et vōs, mīlitēs, estōte fortēs. Hostibus resistite usque ad fīnem—usque ad mortem. Ferte cīvibus salūtem, urbī lībertātem, patriae glōriam.

Sight Translation, p. 251.—Rome, the Eternal City. Rome is an illustrious city. Romulus, its first king, gave the city its name. The Tiber River divides the city. There are other cities in Italy, but Rome is the most famous of them all. Rome is the head of Italy. In this city the Senate was held. The consuls convoked the Senate. In the Senate one consul adopted a plan, the other said nothing. Cicero, on account of fear of the conspiracy, held the Senate in a fortified place. They all came to this place. Cicero comes into the Senate, tells everything, reveals everything; he is unaware of nothing, avoids nothing. Catiline was also in the Senate. He makes no move. He thinks of many things but says nothing.

At the time of Cicero, Roman citizens were proud men. All other men were called barbarians. Roman citizens were living throughout the whole world. Not all barbarians were well disposed to the Roman influence. No Roman citizen was condemned to death. Barbarians, however, had for a long time been condemned to death by the order of the praetor. To avoid death men often claimed to be Roman citizens.

Afterward the city of Rome became Christian. All Christians understood that Rome was the head of the Catholic Church. St. Peter and St. Paul suffered death for Christ in the city of Rome. Rome is even up to our own time the head of the Catholic Church, and always will be. Pius the Twelfth is father of all the Christians in the world. He often gives messages "to the city and to the world." He has supreme authority in the Catholic Church. He holds Peter's place; nay more, the place of Christ Himself.

In this manner we are all Roman citizens. Once St. Peter shouted, "I am a Roman citizen!" All we Catholics say, "Hail, eternal Rome! We are Roman citizens!" May we be good citizens of eternal Rome!

Answer in Latin, p. 252.—1. What kind of city is Rome? (Rōma est urbs clāra.) 2. Who gave Rome its name? (Romulus Rōmae nōmen dēdit.) 3. Are there other cities in Italy? (Aliae sunt urbēs in Italiā.) 4. There are no cities more famous than Rome, are there? (Nulla urbs clārior quam Rōma est; ea est omnium clārissima.) 5. What city is the first city of Italy? (Rōma est caput Italiae.) 6. In what city was the Senate held? (Rōmae senātus habēbātur.) 7. Who convoked the Senate? (Cōnsulēs senātum convocābant.) 8. How many consuls were there? (Duo cōnsulēs erant.) 9. What did one of the consuls do in the Senate? (In senātū alter cōnsul cōnsilium cēpit.) 10. Why did Cicero fortify the place for holding Senate? (Cicerō propter conjūrātiōnis timōrem locum habendī senātus mūnīvit.) 11. What did Cicero do in the Senate? (Cicerō in senātū omnia dīxit, omnia patefēcit.) 12. What did Catiline say? (Catilīna nihil dīxit.) 13. What did the Romans call other men? (Rōmānī omnēs aliōs hominēs barbarōs vocābant.) 14. Where did Roman citizens live? (Cīvēs Rōmānī in tōtō orbe terrae vīvēbant.) 15. How did the barbarians feel about the power of the Romans? (Nōn omnēs barbarī eī fāvēbant.) 16. Roman citizens were not subject to the death penalty, were they? (Nullus cīvis Rōmānus ad mortem dūcēbātur.) 17. How were barbarians condemned to death? (Jussū praetōris barbarī ad mortem dūcēbantur.) 18. How did they often escape death? (Ad mortem vītandam saepe dīxērunt sē esse cīvēs Rōmānōs.) 19. Rome became Christian, did she not? (Ita, urbs Rōma facta est Chrīstiāna.) 20. What city is the first city of the Catholic Church? (Rōma est caput ecclesiae Catholicae.) 21. In what city did Peter and Paul suffer? (In urbe Rōmā passī sunt.) 22. Why did they suffer? (Propter Chrīstum passī sunt.) 23. Is Rome the first city of the Catholic Church? (Est.)

24. Who is father of all Christians? (Pius duodecimus est pater omnium Chrīstiānōrum.) 25. Why are his letters written "to the city and to the world"? (Litterae ējus dantur "urbī et orbī" quod pater omnium Chrīstiānōrum in orbe terrārum est.) 26. Who has supreme authority in the Catholic Church? (Pius duodecimus suprēmam auctōritātem in ecclesiā Catholicā habet.) 27. Whose place does Pius the Twelfth hold? (Locum tenet Petrī et ipsīus Chrīstī.) 28. In this way are we not all Roman citizens? (Nōs hōc modō omnēs sumus cīvēs Rōmānī.) 29. What did Paul once shout? (Clāmāvit: "Cīvis Rōmānus sum!") 30. In this respect is Rome eternal? (Rōma hōc modō aeterna est.) 31. What do all we Catholics openly say? (Dīcimus, "Ave Rōma aeterna! Cīvēs Rōmānī sumus!")

Lesson 8

Exercise 28.—1 Although the consul spoke in the Senate for two hours, not everyone heard him. (*Duās hōrās,* Gr. 919.) 2. On the third day, however, he spoke for one hour only. (*Ūnam tantum hōram,* Gr. 919.) 3. Within five days he will speak before the Roman people. (*Quīnque diēbus,* Gr. 922.) 4. Many years ago our fathers fortified this place. (*Abhinc multōs annōs,* Gr. 923.) 5. Catiline desired to set out for the camp after a certain number of days. (*Certīs post diēbus,* Gr. 924, 1.) 6. Roman cavalry came to Cicero's home a little before dawn. (*Ante lūcem,* Gr. 924, 2.) 7. After a few days he fortified and strengthened his home. (*Paucīs post diēbus,* Gr. 924, 1.) 8. After Caesar's death civil wars threatened the Roman republic for many years. (*Post mortem,* Gr. 924, 3; *multōs annōs,* Gr. 919.) 9. The leader exhorted the people for three hours. Then finally he was silent, for his voice could now no longer be heard. (*Trēs hōrās,* Gr. 919.) 10. The Roman forces had for many years been in difficulties. (*Multōs jam annōs,* Gr. 919.) 11. What you did last night and the night before I do not know. (*Superiōre nocte,* Gr. 920.) 12. All Catiline's friends were standing armed that day. (*Illō diē,* Gr. 920.) 13. The night before last an unbelievable outrage was discovered. (*Superiōre nocte,* Gr. 920.) 14. Although you were at Laeca's house that night, you could accomplish nothing. (*Illā nocte,* Gr. 920.) 15. At the same time he exhorted the rest of the allies. (*Eōdem tempore,* Gr. 920.) 16. Although they often punished him, he always remained silent. 17. Private citizens often suffer on account of public disasters. 18. Throughout his whole life the consul wanted to save Roman power from both public ruin and private disaster. 19. At dawn he called his friend, thanked him, and sent him away. (*Prīmā lūce,* Gr.

920.) 20. Common disaster is often a means of uniting men. 21. Although in time of war men often desire a common good, in time of peace they want [only] their own individual good. (*Tempore bellī, tempore pācis,* Gr. 920.) 22. Christ lived a public life for three years. (*Trēs annōs,* Gr. 919.) 23. Three years afterward the enemy put him to death. (*Post trēs annōs,* Gr. 924, 3.) 24. For how many hours was Christ on the cross? (*Quot hōrās,* Gr. 919.) 25. But at the third hour Christ cried out with a loud voice, "My Father, into Thy hands I commend my spirit." (*Tertiā hōrā,* Gr. 920.) 26. And bowing His head, He sent forth His spirit. 27. Darkness fell at the time Christ died. (*Eō tempore,* Gr. 920.) 28. But on the third day, Christ, master of life, rose again. (*Tertiā diē,* Gr. 920.) 29. We must be very grateful to God and to His Son. 30. The people thanked Cicero for his carefulness. 31. We ought always to preserve the reputation of our friends. 32. The consul said a few things to those men who might feel the same. 33. For a long time now this dreadful ruin of the state has threatened the citizens. 34. The leader killed the consul with a sword. 35. Citizens often defend themselves by personal watchfulness rather than by a public guard. 36. The companions recently united in crime are a domestic plague. 37. But Christ fled from their hands; for His time had not yet come. 38. Two Roman horsemen promised they would kill me that very night a little before dawn. (*Illā ipsā nocte,* Gr. 920; *paulō ante lūcem,* Gr. 924, 2.) 39. He stood in the assembly for ten hours. (*Decem hōrās,* Gr. 919.) 40. Have you ever spoken in the Senate for three hours? (*Trēs hōrās,* Gr. 919.)

Exercise 29.—1. Abhinc quīnque diēs mē vindicāre voluistī. 2. Trībus diēbus facinus tuum patefaciēmus. 3. Duābus diēbus ante proelium Catilīna Rōmā discessit. 4. Propter difficultātem domesticam quīnque diēs exspectāvērunt. 5. Post Caesaris mortem bella domestica Rōmae impendēbant. 6. Trēs hōrās populī extrā senātum stetērunt. Dux tandem exiit. 7. Eīs nōn nūper locūtus erat. 8. Vir quīdam Catilīnae cōnsilia nōbis nuntiāvit. 9. In bellō hominēs hostēs vindicāre cupiunt. 10. Diē sextā facinus comperērunt. 11. Diē octāvā scelus vindicātum est. 12. Decem diēs mīlitēs contrā calamitātem domesticam sē dēfendērunt. 13. Prīmā lūce amīcus mē vocāvit. 14. An arbitrāris dūcēs reī pūblicae dē hīs turpitūdinibus domesticīs umquam silēre posse? 15. Cōnsul decem annōs in vītā pūblicā fuerat; reliquōs annōs vītae suae ab oculīs populī fūgēbant. 16. In bellō difficultātēs domesticae complūribus cīvibus impendent. 17. ~~Praetōris~~ famam jam diū nesciēbant. 18. Quae turpitūdō ab coetibus vestrīs umquam āfuit? 19. Sī facinus factum esset, fama dē eō per oppidum tōtum audīta esset; nēmō cīvēs ā difficultāte impendente vindicāre potuisset.

Exercise 30 [Sermō Pātris Iratī in Fīlium Improbum].—Jam diū tēcum plānē loquī volō. Nunc diūtius silēre nōn possum. Vērō obscūrē nōn agam, sed omnia quae sciō tibi dīcam.

Ubi proximā nocte fueris, quōs amīcōs tēcum habueris, quae loca adieris mē ignōrāre arbitrāris? Multōrum oculī et aurēs tē nōn sentientem speculantur. Nēque nox tenebrīs nec prīvāta domūs parietibus coetūs tuōs nēfariōs continēre possunt. Omnia illustrantur, omnia ērumpunt.

Mūtā jam istam mentem, fīlī mī. Mihi crēde; oblīvīscere hūjus modī vītam. Quam diū patientiam meam hanc turpitūdinem domesticam passūram esse arbitrāris?

Fuit quondam ista in tē virtūs ut quae imperārentur agerēs. Rēs nūper sē mūtāvērunt et difficultātēs domesticae impendent. Tibi imperium acre et grave dō: Hūjusmodī rēs numquam iterum facienda est. Tē diūtius nōn monēbō. Verbum sapientī sat est. Ego dīxī.

General Review Exercises

Exercise 31.—1. Cicero had a severe and weighty decree of the Senate. 2. By a similar decree of the Senate other consuls had led enemies of the state to death. 3. According to this senatorial decree Catiline should long ago have been led to death. 4. We have no senatorial decree of this kind. 5. Cicero had great authority; the other consul had none. 6. The authority of the Senate moved Catiline not at all. 7. Men are put to death by the authority of the state. 8. All authority comes from God. 9. One of the good citizens told me this. 10. The consul was moving the goods of all the citizens from the city. 11. On account of fear all the citizens came to the fortified place. 12. He told all this to the citizens; nor had he overlooked a single thing. 13. Brave citizens often suffer death for the sovereignty of the state. 14. I am a Roman citizen. 15. They asked him whether he was a Roman citizen. 16. The band of enemies wanted to kill all good citizens. 17. They did not kill the public enemy, did they? 18. One is God, the Father of all. 19. "I desire," said Cicero, "I desire, Gentlemen of the Senate, that the Senate have great authority." 20. My father is a serious and brave man. 21. Patience is a great virtue, is it not? 22. Catiline had no virtue. 23. On that very day their fathers came. 24. Day and night all the citizens suffered on account of one man. 25. All good Christians suffer with Christ. 26. I will at some time come with you. 27. For all cities seem the same to me. 28. All those who had come into the Senate were serious and brave. 29. He took a long dart. 30. He made for the other city with a numerous band. 31. No night was of this kind. 32. Were all the citizens unaware that a conspiracy had been formed? By no means. 33. Did Cicero call the Senate together in one place? 34. They placed authority in one man. 35. On account of the death of one man, Christ, all men have a place in heaven. 36. He resembled his father. 37. No man has had, has, or will have the virtue of Christ. 38. For Christ is God. 39. Catiline stood in the assembly with a weapon. 40. Cicero betook himself to the Senate with a great band. 41. In what city do we live? 42. In this venerable body [of the Senate] are enemies of the state. 43. But for a long time a band of enemies has continued to live in the state. 44. All authority was vested in the other consul. 45. Christ said all things plainly. 46. In Herod's council Christ said nothing. 47. For the Senate had decreed that the consuls should see to it that the state suffered no harm. 48. His father will not suffer madness of this sort. 49. But in this state private individuals condemned citizens to death. 50. For I see that there is no other way. 51. What, then, is virtue? 52. Nor was Catiline a man of this sort. 53. In the beginning God made heaven and earth. 54. What did God make on the second day? 55. Was not man made from the earth? 56. God saw that all things were good, did He not? 57. All men do not think that all things are good, do they? 58. While Christ was living on earth He both did and said good things. 59. Christ did not overlook the authority of the state, but rather noted it openly. 60. Has Christ a higher authority over us than the state?

Exercise 32.—1. Catiline lived, and lived not to lay aside but rather to strengthen his brazenness. 2. But for a certain reason Cicero was not yet led to do that which he ought long before to have done. 3. There was a camp established in Italy against the Roman people; the number of the enemy was increasing day by day; its (the camp's) commander and the leader of the enemy was Catiline himself. 4. That fellow had come within the walls and even into the Senate. 5. He was daily striving for the internal destruction of the state. 6. He wanted to ravage all of Italy. 7. The consul, the Senate, the citizens, the Roman people, the city of Rome, all Italy were in danger on account of that one man. 8. But Cicero wanted to be merciful; amid such great dangers to the state he did not wish to put Catiline to death. 9. Cicero perceived that no one was unaware of the conspiracy of that man. 10. Yet he told no one. 11. Catiline made for the camp with a band of wicked men. 12. Desperate men were every day being won over to Catiline's cause.

13. Among such a large number of Romans some wicked and desperate citizens felt that Catiline was a good leader. 14. But I had at no time seen such authority, such endurance, such courage. 15. I understood all this. 16. Christ knew that the Jews had taken counsel against Him. 17. On that very day Christ suffered. 18. The night before, He said, "Father, Thy will be done." 19. "What do you think of the state?" said Cicero. 20. The Holy Spirit strengthens all Christians. 21. No man was so wicked and so desperate that he did not see that a conspiracy had been formed. 22. Would that the Roman republic had escaped destruction! 23. I am able to live with you no longer. 24. Cicero defended himself not by means of a public guard, but by his own diligence. 25. The leader of the enemy was within the walls and even in the Senate.

Exercise 33.—1. Quam diū Rōmam ōderis? 2. Nescīmus quam diū Rōmam ōsūrus sit. 3. Jam diū Rōmam ōdistī. 4. Jam dūdum cīvibus īnsidiābātur. 5. Nōs quīntum jam diem istum vīvere patimur. 6. Dīxī ego īdem eum vītae omnium nostrum īnsidiārī. 7. Sunt quī vītae omnium cīvium īnsidientur. 8. Cicerō ipse hoc dīxit. 9. Dīxit sē Rōmā ēgressūrum esse. 10. Cicerō negāvit eōs Rōmae jam diūtius permanēre posse. 11. Conjūrātōrēs suī cōnservandī causā fūgērunt. 12. Custōdibus imperāvit ut domum suam dēfenderent. 13. Exīvitne Catilīna Rōmā? 14. Num istum metuis? 15. Nōnne haec dīxit? 16. An exspectās ut mē interficiās? 17. Quis nostrum cōnsilia ējus ignōrat? 18. Rogāvit utrum Catilīna ex urbe egressūrus esset necne. 19. Exībisne ex urbe annōn? 20. Quaesīvit num senātus Catilīnam metueret. 21. Scīmus quibuscum in proximīs comitiīs fuerīs. 22. Profectusne est ad castra? 23. Eratne nūper Catilīna Rōmae? 24. Quandō Rōmā proficīscētur? 25. Fēcēruntne iter quīnque diēs? 26. Rōmā tertiā hōrā exiit. 27. Mīlitēs Rōmam contendērunt. 28. Erat calamitās magna in Galliā. 29. Per prōvinciam iter fēcit. 30. Decem diēbus exībit. 31. Post complūrēs diēs interfectī sunt. 32. Paulō ante lūcem nuntius advēnit. 33. Multīs post annīs complūrēs hominēs eum laudāvērunt. 34. Abhinc quīnque diēs Catilīna Rōmā exiit. 35. Multōs jam diēs Cicerōnem audīmus.

Exercise 34.—1. Quam diū igitur Rōmae manēbis? 2. Nōnne praesidium urbis tē movet? 3. Nōnne oculōs omnium bonōrum verēris? 4. Nōnne Catilīna sēnsit Cicerōnem cōnsilia sua intellegere? 5. Tamen in senātum venīre audet. 6. Rogāsne num coetuī adfuerit? 7. Nōnne senātus et cōnsulēs haec intellēxērunt? 8. Suntne quī Catilīnam dēfenderent? 9. Nōnne Catilīna diū contrā urbem machinābātur? 10. Rogāvit Catilīnam num exitūrus esset ex urbe. 11. "Ēgredere," inquit, "patent portae." 12. Dīxistī tē mē timēre. Dīxistī tē mē ōdisse. Tū īdem dīxistī fore ut interficerer. 13. Sciō quid tū et tuī proximā nocte fēcerītis. 14. Arbitrārisne mē ignōrāre quid cōnsiliī cēperīs? 15. Quīnque diēbus ante proelium Catilīna Rōmae erat. 16. Ūnō post diē interfectus est. 17. Dīxit sē sē dēfendere. 18. Quisquam Rōmae erat quī tē nōn timēret? 19. Nemō tam perditus erat quī hostēs reī pūblicae dēfenderet. 20. Haec omnia duābus hōrīs comperī. 21. Dubitāsne in exilium īre? 22. Mūnīvitne domum suam firmiōribus praesidiīs? 23. Paulō ante lūcem Rōmam vēnit. 24. Rogāvit num dubitāret in exilium īre. 25. Haec moneō.

Exercise 35.—1. Rōmam profiscīscere. 2. Ēgredere ex urbe. 3. Per prōvinciam iter fāc. 4. Tribus diēbus veniam. 5. Abhinc quattuor annōs interfectus est. 6. Tribus diēbus eum inveniēmus. 7. Rogāvit num Rōmam vēnisset. 8. Abhinc quattuor diēs Rōmam vēnērunt. 9. Eratne domī? 10. Vīditne quemquam? 11. Quem vīdit? 12. Sunt quī tē nōn metuant. 13. Haec jam prīdem cupiēbat. 14. Tertiā hōrā insidiās comperit. 15. Trēs diēs exspectāvit. 16. Rogāvit utrum ventūrī essent necne. 17. Ubi erant castra? 18. Num negāre audēs? 19. Aderatne quisquam? 20. Discēdat suam quisque in domum. 21. Num quisquam est quī haec crēdat? 22. Nōlī timēre. 23. Hōc perīculō nōs līberā. 24. Nescīvī quanta essent castra. 25. Nesciunt ubi sint castra. 26. Nescīvērunt ubi essent castra. 27. In senātum quīntō diē vēnit. 28. Scīvit quī conjūrātī essent. 29. Nescīvit quandō ventūrī essent. 30. Nescīvit ubi conventūrī essent.

Lesson 9

Exercise 36.—1. I say that you come a little before dawn. (*Venīre*, Gr. 897, 885.) 2. I say that you came a little before dawn. (*Vēnisse*, Gr. 897, 886.) 3. I say that you will come a little before dawn. (*Ventūrum esse*, Gr. 897, 887.) 4. My parents said that they were leaving the city. (*Relinquere*, Gr. 897, 885.) 5. My parents said that they had left the city. (*Relīquisse*, Gr. 897, 886.) 6. My parents said that they would leave the city. (*Relictūrōs esse*, Gr. 897, 887.) 7. Cicero thought that Catiline would depart from the city. (*Profectūrum esse*, Gr. 897, 887.) 8. A certain horseman promised that he would kill Cicero in his bed. (*Interfectūrum esse*, Gr. 897, 887.) 9. But Cicero denied that he had been wounded. (*Vulnerātum esse*, Gr. 897, 886.) 10. The consuls think that the state has been freed from fear. (*Esse līberātam*, Gr. 897, 886.) 11. The leader knew that a large part of the cavalry had been left within the walls. (*Relictam esse*, Gr. 897, 886.) 12. It has been handed down that the kings of the Romans were good. (*Fuisse*, Gr. 901, 886.) 13. The consul is said to be leaving the city. (*Exīre*, Gr. 902, 886.) 14. Cicero

seems to be moved by fear. (*Movērī*, Gr. 902, 885.) 15. The Senate and
the consuls decided to dismiss the enemy. (*Dīmittī*, Gr. 903, 885.)
16. Who is there who endures this? (*Ferat*, Gr. 634.) 17. There were in
the Senate some who pondered the destruction of the state. (*Cōgitārent*,
Gr. 634.) 18. The soldiers said they preferred to die rather than go into
exile. (*Morī, īre*, Gr. 640.) 19. We cannot long be without the sight of
our parents. (*Carēre*, Gr. 889.) 20. I suspected that his parents killed
him. 21. We saw a just man slipping away from the throng of citizens.
(*Ēlābī*, Gr. 897, 885.) 22. We are not unaware, fellow citizens, that we
are being overwhelmed by the enemy. (*Opprimī*, Gr. 897, 885.) 23. I
prefer to withdraw from the crowd with my friends. (*Concēdere*, Gr.
640.) 24. The boys saw their parents at a distance. 25. Christ, however,
promised that He would send the Holy Spirit.

Exercise 37.—1. Cōnsul dīcit sē audāciam ējus modī diūtius ferre
nōn posse. 2. Chrīstus dīxit sē hominēs ex tenebrīs in lūcem ductūrum
esse. 3. Sunt quī equitēs Rōmānōs dīmittere nōlint. 4. Dīxit sē ipsum
odium pārentum suōrum nōn suspicārī. 5. Īvit usque ad portās; nōn
autem ēlāpsus est. 6. Suntne in hōc senātō quī vastāre Rōmam, moenia
ējus, domōs ējus cupiant? 7. Dīcis hōs virōs in armīs etiam jam esse.
8. Negāvit sē magnam equitum partem intra moenia relictūrum esse.
9. Pollicitī sunt sē urbem ā metū līberātūrōs esse. 10. Dīcō hōs sociōs
criminis hāc ipsā nocte vēnisse. 11. Sunt quī Deum laudent propter
timōrem. 12. Aspectus frequentiae mē semper opprimit. 13. Dīcō mē
carēre pārentibus nōn posse. 14. Dīcō hostēs in armīs fuisse. 15. Dīcō
hostēs in armīs futūrōs esse. 16. Arbitrātī sunt populum audāciā unīus
hominis līberātōs esse. 17. Arbitrātī sunt Catilīnam proeliō vulnerātum
esse. 18. Dīcō pārentēs meōs semper justōs futūrōs esse. 19. Cōnsul
quidem dīcitur ā frequentiā ēlāpsus esse. 20. Ille putātur suspectus esse
odiī. 21. Audiō frequentiam post judicium concessisse. 22. Rērum
aspectūs judicium nostrum saepe impediunt. 23. Nihil vidēre poterāmus;
diēs obscūra erat et dōmus lūce carēbat. 24. Imperātor arbitrātus est sē
hostēs opprimere posse, sed illī nōn concessērunt. 25. Oportet quidem
pārentēs bonōs comperīre quibus puerī suī careant. 26. Dēbēmus dē
amīcīs nostrīs loquī sīcut eōs dē nōbīs loquī malumus. 27. Nōn justum
est ōdisse (odiō habēre) pārentēs.

Exercise 38.—Model: For I will now speak to you, not as one
seeming to be moved by righteous enmity, but by mercy, which is in no
way your due.

1. Sīc enim jam agam, nōn ut metū permōtus esse videar, sed amōre
patriae.

2. Tē enim jam ad mortem dūcī jubēbō, nōn ut patiāris sicut dēbēs, sed ut rēs pūblica metū careat.

3. Sīc enim jam Deum laudābō, nōn ut peccātor timōre commōtus, quō dēbeō, sed ut fīlius amōre, quī Deō certissimē dēbētur.

4. Sīc enim jam tēcum, fīlī mī, loquar, nōn ut īra permōtus esse videar, quā dēbeō, sed dīligentiā dē fāmā tuā, quae tibi mihique esse carissima dēbet.

Exercise 39.—1. In what spirit, think you, should you suffer the people's fear? 2. The consul bore well all these things. 3. I said likewise that I would leave the city shortly before. 4. The consul ordered the enemy to leave the city. 5. "Since this is so," said Cicero, "proceed with what you have begun; leave the city at last, the gates are open, go." 6. Depart from the city; free the state from fear, go! 7. The allies who had assembled at Laeca's left his home. 8. I heard that a Roman horseman had been sent to me. 9. Lead out with you all your wicked companions. 10. When he knew that the meeting had been adjourned, Cicero fortified and strengthened his home by stronger guards. 11. Three times Peter denied that he knew Christ. 12. He had promised that he would follow the Lord even to the end. 13. The just man indeed prefers the will of God. 14. The voice can wound men's minds just as the sword their bodies. 15. Would that we were free of every care! 16. The two companions conjectured that the night would be dark. 17. Catiline had come into the Senate shortly before. 18. We ought always to have in mind the supreme welfare of the state. 19. The best and most famous citizens had left the city out of fear. 20. We all know that Catiline has apportioned the sections of the city among his companions. 21. The Roman horsemen were the best and most illustrious men. 22. Hatred, as we all know, hinders man's judgment.

From the Roman Missal, p. 267.—From the Proper of the Saints. A reading from the Book of Exodus: The Lord God said this: Behold I will send my angel, who shall go before thee, and keep thee in thy journey, and bring thee unto the place that I have prepared. Heed him, and hear his voice and do not think him worthy of scorn: for he will not forgive when thou hast sinned, and my name is in him. But if thou wilt hear his voice, and do all that I speak, I will be an enemy to thy enemies, and will strike them that strike thee, and my angel shall go before thee.

The continuation of the holy Gospel according to St. Matthew: At that time the disciples came to Jesus, saying, "Who, think you, is greater in the kingdom of heaven?" And Jesus, calling a little child to him, set him in their midst, and said, "Amen I say to you, unless you change and become like little children, you shall not enter into the kingdom of heaven. . . . See that you do not despise one of these little ones, for I tell you, their angels in heaven always behold the face of my Father in heaven."

Lesson 10

Exercise 40.—1. After the investigation, the enemies of the fatherland were led to prison. (*Quaestiōne factā,* Gr. 912.) 2. Although they did not adjudge them to be worthy of death, yet their friends were not influential enough to snatch them unpunished out of custody. (*Ē custōdiā,* Gr. 916.) 3. He finally returned to his native land; for ten years now he had lived in exile. (*Ad patriam,* Gr. 917.) 4. Charity is the bond of all the virtues. 5. Because he had discovered the conspiracy, Cicero was deserving of every praise. (*Conjūrātiōne compertā,* Gr. 912.) 6. When the leader had died, all his friends silently departed from his house. (*Duce mortuō,* Gr. 912; *domō,* Gr. 916.) 7. Save me, O Lord, from the hands of false friends. (*Dē manū,* Gr. 954.) 8. In Italy there was a camp established against the Roman people. (*In Italiā,* Gr. 915.) 9. In what city do you live? (*In quā urbe,* Gr. 915.) 10. In this most sacred and important legislative body there are some who are not strong enough to employ force. (*In hōc sānctissimō gravissimōque cōnsiliō,* Gr. 915.) 11. How many prisons are there in this state? (*In hāc cīvitāte,* Gr. 915.) 12. In the consulship of Lepidus and Tullus, Catiline stood in the assembly with a weapon. (*Lepidō et Tullō cōnsulibus,* Gr. 912; *in comitiō,* Gr. 915.) 13. He was not, however, able to take weapons away from the camp. (*Ex castrīs,* Gr. 916.) 14. In the temple itself many citizens were silently begging for peace for the fatherland every day. (*Ipsō in templō,* Gr. 915.) 15. The consul commanded the enemy to go out of the city. (*Ex urbe,* Gr. 916.) 16. Who in this crowded assembly, from among your many friends, has spoken with you? (*Ex hāc tantā frequentiā,* Gr. 916.) 17. Depart from the city, Catiline, free the state from fear; depart into exile—if this is the word you are waiting for. (*Ex urbe,* Gr. 916; *metū,* Gr. 766.) 18. But in this state even private individuals often judge false citizens worthy of bonds. (*In hāc rē pūblicā,* Gr. 915.) 19. Let the deceivers depart from the citizens' view and no longer dwell with good men. 20. The man who has already judged himself worthy of custody cannot be far away from the dungeon's chains. 21. When the break was made, all who were in the prison fled to the nearest town. (*Ēruptiōne factā,* Gr. 912.) 22. The Jews threw Peter

into prison; in that same night, however, Peter, under the angel's guid-
ance, was snatched from the chains. (*In carcerem*, Gr. 917; *angelō duce*,
Gr. 912.) 23. Let all wicked and desperate men depart from the temples,
from the buildings and walls of the city, from the state, nay more, from
the fatherland—let them go into exile. (*In exilium*, Gr. 917.) 24. How
often already has that dagger of yours slipped from your hands! (*Dē
manibus tuīs*, Gr. 916.) 25. At midnight, however, the enemy withdrew
silently from the walls. (*Dē mūrīs*, Gr. 916.) 26. A little after the
inquiry was made, the consul came into the Senate. (*Quaestiōne habitā*,
Gr. 912.) 27. Do you not judge that this man ought to be put into
chains? (*In vincula*, Gr. 917.) 28. With all the unpunished gathered
into one place, the careful consul wanted to hold an inquiry. (*Omnibus
impūnītīs convocātīs*, Gr. 912.) 29. Here, here in our number are some
still unpunished who would inflict war on the fatherland. 30. If you
judge this to be true, speak openly; if false, be silent.

Exercise 41.—1. Coetū dīmissō, cōnsul in senātum īvit. 2. Nūllō
tumultū pūblicō concitātō, Cicerō hostēs patriae ad mortem dūxit.
3. Mē cōnsule, Rōma ā magnā perniciē ērepta est. 4. Senātō convocātō,
cōnsul gladiōs ē domibus privātīs collēgit. 5. Nēmō Rōmae est quī tē
dignum custōdiā esse jūdicet. 6. Estne ēlapsus impūnītus ā mīlitum
manibus? 7. Dūc virōs in Italiam. 8. Rōmā discessērunt et in oppidō
fīnitimō habitāvērunt. 9. Nōn poterant dūcere exercitum per prōvinciam. 10. Nōn scīvērunt ubi carcer esset. 11. Post mortem ējus dē
eō multa falsa locūtī sunt. 12. Exercitus in patriam iter fēcit. 13. Quaestiōne impetrātā, cōnsul dīligens complūrēs ē carcere ēripuit. 14. Hostēs
reī pūblicae vinculīs dignī sunt. 15. Omnēs tacitī ā patriā discessērunt.
16. Imperātor nōn valuit in quaestiōne privātā dē mīlitibus vim ad-
hibēre. 17. Rōmae cīvēs scīvērunt quam firmae quaestiōnēs essent.
18. Vinculum amicītiae firmum est. 19. Quī in oppidīs parvīs habitant
saepe tacitī sunt. 20. Ut valēs? Valeō.

Sight Translation, p. 272.—The Mother of the Gracchi, Part 1.
Cornelia was the daughter of Publius Scipio Africanus, who conquered
Hannibal. She became the wife of Tiberius Sempronius Gracchus. They
had two sons, the elder of whom was Tiberius, the younger Gaius.

Once a noblewoman was showing off her jewels to Cornelia. Cornelia
praised them for their beauty, but thereupon called her sons to her and
said, "These are my jewels."

Tiberius Gracchus was a brilliant orator and a courageous soldier. He
was both praised and loved by the Roman people.

In his time throughout the whole of Italy there was a great number of slaves. Many citizens who were not able to live in the country now came into the city and were living in Rome. The Roman state had long since been in great danger. Tiberius Gracchus and his brother Gaius were striving to save the state. They wanted to lead many citizens back to the land from the city and to distribute the public lands, which for a long time had been in the hands of a few. Tiberius' enemies, however, thought that he was fomenting revolution and for this reason killed him.

Answer in Latin, p. 273.—1. Whose daughter was Cornelia? ((ornēlia erat fīlia Pūblii Scīpiōnis Āfricānī.) 2. **Whom had Publius Scipio** conquered? (Pūblius Scīpio Hannibalem vīcerat.) 3. Whose wife did Cornelia become? (Uxor Tiberiō Semprōniō Gracchō facta est.) 4. How many sons did they have? (Duōs fīliōs habuērunt.) 5. Who was the elder and who was the younger? (Tiberius senior erat, Gājus minor.) 6. Were not the noblewoman's jewels beautiful? (Ita, pulchra erant.) 7. Did Cornelia have jewels? (Fīlii ōrnāmenta sua erant.) 8. What sort of orator was Tiberius? What sort of soldier? (Tiberius erat ōrātor clārus et mīles fortis.) 9. In the time of Tiberius were the citizens able to live in the country? (Nōn potuērunt.) 10. Why not? (Quia agrōs nōn habēbant aut quia ea quae vītam sustinent in agrīs invenīre nōn poterant.) 11. Where did they go? (Rōmam sē contulērunt.) 12. The Roman state was in danger, wasn't it? (Ita, magnō in perīculō versābātur.) 13. What did the Gracchi brothers wish to do? (Studēbant rem pūblicam servāre.) 14. Who owned the fields? (Agrī in manibus paucōrum hominum erant.) 15. It wasn't easy to lead the citizens from the city back to the land, was it? (Difficile fuit redūcere cīvēs ex urbe in agrōs.) 16. Do you think that the Gracchi did indeed foment revolution? (Nōn putō Gracchōs novīs rēbus studuisse.) 17. Tiberius was not justly killed, was he? (Tiberius minimē jūre occīsus est.)

Lesson 11

Exercise 42.—1. In the Senate you must almost shout if you want to be heard. (*Clāmandum*, Gr. 881.) 2. Cicero was speaking about the necessity of avoiding the hatred of honest citizens. (*Vītandā*, Gr. 867.) 3. At Rome many young men were eager to fight. (*Pugnandī*, Gr. 864.) 4. For the sake of fortifying the city, the rest of the citizens offered themselves. (*Mūniendae*, Gr. 872.) 5. All young men seem to understand with difficulty that there is a time for speech and a time for silence. (*Loquendī* and *tacendī*, Gr. 864.) 6. Men are able to overcome unpopularity by thought. (*Cōgitandō*, Gr. 864.) 7. I thought you would be most diligent at guarding. (*Custōdiendum*, Gr. 864.) 8. His eagerness is scarcely to be given up. (*Dēpōnendum*, Gr. 880.) 9. We must fear a storm of hatred. (*Metuenda*, Gr. 882.) 10. Parents are more dear by far than all other friends. 11. But it is too much to ask that you should dread the penalties of the law, or give up your ambitions at this moment of national crisis. (*Postulandum*, Gr. 878.) 12. We should often recall to our minds the thought of death. (*Revocanda*, Gr. 880.) 13. He came to Rome to live. (*Vīvendī*, Gr. 864.) 14. Learn this, all of you, that envy must be put aside. (*Dēpōnendam*, Gr. 880.) 15. Christ, hear us; Christ, give heed to us. 16. Several buildings were destroyed by the storm. 17. Bad will must be destroyed. (*Frangenda*, Gr. 878.) 18. It is scarcely ever necessary for us to surrender to circumstances. (*Cēdendum*, Gr. 882.) 19. They were sent to fortify the city. (*Mūniendam*, Gr. 870.) 20. We must go out. (*Eundum*, Gr. 882.) 21. The fatherland should be served. (*Serviendum*, Gr. 881.) 22. You ask me whether God should be served. (*Deō serviendum*, Gr. 881.) 23. I must be silent concerning these troubles. (*Tacendum*, Gr. 882.) 24. He said the people must be served by the consul. (*Populō ā cōnsule serviendum*, Gr. 882.) 25. He was scarcely unskilled in speaking. (*Loquendī*, Gr. 864.)

Exercise 43.—1. Invidia nōbīs semper vītanda est. 2. Tempus est loquendī, tempus tacendī. 3. Studium hūjus adulēscentis in difficultātibus vincendīs laudandum est. 4. Parentēs nostrī cārī clāmābănt, sed propter tempestātem exaudīrī nōn poterant. 5. Tempestās idōnea erat ad proficīscendum. 6. Ab adulēscēnte patriae cārae relinquendum erat. 7. Ceterī cīvēs honestōrum ab exiliō revocandī sunt. 8. Nōs vix vōcem ējus exaudīre poterāmus. 9. Hōc locō clāmandum est, sī exaudīrī vīs. 10. Dīligentia semper postulanda est. 11. Nihil audāciam Catilīnae frangere poterat dum Rōmae erat. 12. Numquam hostibus ā mīlite bonō cēdendum est. 13. Quod ā cōnsule agitur nōbīs dīligenter percipiendum est.

Exercise 44.—1. Doesn't this well-fortified meeting place of the Senate make the slightest impression upon you? 2. You still live to redouble your effrontery. 3. Will this deserve my fear? 4. His courage is far more to be admired. 5. They fled for the sake of their own safety. 6. We must be very grateful to the immortal gods. 7. You prepared a band for the sake of killing the leading men. 8. Surely you don't think you ought to leave your house? 9. His effrontery, fellow citizens of Rome, is not to be borne. 10. You have gone with me in order to rid yourself of suspicion. 11. He is strong in punishing. 12. That you should change your fell purpose at last is too much to ask. 13. I will not give you a single hour to live. 14. He called together several desperate young men to fortify the city. 15. He sent an envoy for the sake of avoiding war. 16. He was always strong in his devotion to public speaking. 17. We must fight with him. 18. I will bring it about that you need no longer fear. 19. This is the best time for fighting. 20. Catiline is eager to seize the city. 21. He is very careful at guarding. 22. It is time for action, not speech. 23. This misfortune must be borne with great patience. 24. The battle had to be fought in the mountains. 25. Cicero should not be forgotten. 26. The children should be spared by the soldiers. 27. We must go. 28. The consul persuaded the Senate.

Exercise 45.—Model: I shall easily persuade the men whose hands and weapons I have for a long time scarcely kept from you to pursue you even to the gates, as you leave behind the things you have long desired to destroy.

1. Quī tē ad mortem dūcere jam diū cupiunt, eōsdem facile addūcam ut tē aliquandō populō Rōmānō locūtum laudārent.

2. Quī Germānōs jam diū timēbant, eōsdem Caesar facile addūxit ut sē legiōnēs contrā hostēs dūcentem fortiter sequerentur.

Exercise 46.—1. Mentēs nostrae cōnfirmandae sunt cōgitandō dē hīs nōbilibus virīs. 2. Deō ā nōbīs serviendum est. 3. Hoc est optimum tempus reī pūblicae hōc perīculō līberandae. 4. Quae dīxit nōbīs audiendae sunt. 5. Catilīna improbus Rōmā Cicerōnī dēpellendus erat. 6. Rēx fortis Rōmānōs nōn timēbat. 7. Hoc nōn admīrandum est. 8. Virōs mīsit ad urbem capiendam. 9. Vincendum nōbīs est aut moriendum. 10. Parātus ad dīcendum est. 11. Furor ējus nōn ferendus est. 12. Līberīs ā nōbīs parcendum est. (Līberē nōbīs cōnservandī sunt.) 13. Ad Gallōs incitandōs missus est. 14. Hoc nōn metuendum est. 15. Interficiendus est. 16. Cīvēs perniciōsī reprimendī sunt. 17. Īnsidiae ējus vītandae sunt. 18. Rēs pūblica perīculīs līberanda est. 19. Cicerō omnibus hominibus laudandus est. 20. Bellum nōbīs vītandum est.

Exercise 47.—1. Huic virō ā nōbīs crēdendum est. 2. Ille adulēscēns laudandus est. 3. Cicerō dīxit virtūtem laudandam esse. 4. Cicerō semper parātus erat ad dīcendum. 5. Servī captī nōbīs postulandī sunt. 6. Hoc bonum tempus est populī convocandī. 7. Haec urbs eīs numquam vastanda est. 8. Frangendus est ā nōbīs quasi pestis esset. 9. Hoc ad senātum nōn dēferendum est. 10. Tibi eundum est in exilium, Catilīna. 11. Hoc quidem nōn est postulandum. 12. Lēgum poenae tibi pertimēscendae sunt. 13. Caedis cīvium eī oblīvīscendum est. 14. Patriae cārae vīdendae causā vēnērunt. 15. Adulēscentibus ā parentibus nōn semper persuādendum est; eīs saepe imperandum est. 16. Deō ab omnibus hominibus ubique et semper serviendum est. 17. Studium adulēscēntium nōn frangendum est dummodo continērī possit.

From the Roman Missal, p. 279.—From the Ordinary of the Mass. I believe in one God, the Father almighty, maker of heaven and earth, [and] of all things visible and invisible. And in one Lord Jesus Christ, the only-begotten Son of God, born of the Father before all ages. God of God; light of light; true God of true God. Begotten, not made; [being of] one substance with the Father, by whom all things were made. Who for us men, and for our salvation, came down from heaven. And was made flesh by the Holy Spirit, of the Virgin Mary; and was made man. He was crucified also for us, suffered under Pontius Pilate, and was buried. And the third day He rose again according to the Scriptures; and ascended into heaven, and sitteth at the right hand of the Father. And He shall come again with glory to judge both the living and the dead; of whose kingdom there shall be no end. And I believe in the Holy Spirit, the Lord and giver of life, who proceedeth from the Father and the Son. Who together with the Father and the Son is adored and glorified; who spoke by the prophets. And in one, holy, catholic, and apostolic Church. I confess one baptism for the remission of sins. And I look for the resurrection of the dead. And the life of the world to come. Amen.

Lesson 12

Exercise 48.—1. A little praise always brings men joy and delight. 2. Brief pleasure oftens brings forth great pain. 3. Christ sits at the right hand of the Father. 4. All the arms and weapons were snatched from the enemy by impious robbery. 5. But if he had sent ahead the upright and courageous Roman soldiers, the citizens would never have been stirred up by our enemies. 6. Surely you were not invited by your excellent friends? 7. Would that our city were not being ravaged by war rather than by brigandage. 8. The courageous Romans equipped themselves in a short time for routing the enemy. 9. All the young men were accustomed to train daily. 10. But if he has cast himself out and taken with him his confreres, he will bring about the final removal of this plague from the republic. 11. If the enemy of the fatherland is hurried away into exile, he can no longer enjoy the pleasure of friendship and the delights of home. 12. The excellent Cicero transferred his enemies to the right-hand part of the Senate. 13. God should always and everywhere be revered by all men.

Exercise 49.—1. What sort of state have we? 2. What crime was ever alien to you? 3. In what spirit, then, do you think you ought to suffer this [rebuff]? 4. The Senate decreed that the consul should see to it that the state suffered no harm. 5. But for a certain reason I have not yet done that which I should have done long ago. 6. You shall live so long as there remains anyone who dares to defend you. 7. The consul said that he could see present in the Senate certain ones who were with Catiline. 8. Cicero asked whether Catiline hesitated to do at the consul's command what he had already been doing of his own free will. 9. There is no one who does not fear the desperate man, no one who does not hate him. 10. Or do you fear unpopularity? 11. On account of fear of unpopularity and danger the praetors betook themselves to a fortified place. 12. "He who is not with Me," Christ said, "is against Me." 13. There was no hope even of a short peace. 14. But if it were so, I should think unpopularity gained by courageous action to be glory, not unpopularity. 15. I will say little of the minds of those who feel this same way. 16. It is robbery to seize another's goods. 17. We exercise our faith by believing. 18. The enemy was preparing swords, weapons, and arms against the fatherland. 19. Stir up the desperate citizens. Inflict war on the fatherland. 20. In such a multitude of citizens I neither heard nor saw any friend. 21. By the care of his parents a young man is saved from every evil. 22. Catiline had fallen in with a gang of desperadoes. 23. The brave scarcely think of flight. 24. Listen carefully to what I shall say, I beg you, and let it sink deep into your souls and minds. 25. If I had said the same thing to this excellent youth, the Senate of its own accord would long since have laid violent hands upon me, their consul, in this very temple. 26. If you go into exile of your own accord, all your associates will leave the city with you. 27. If I had punished this man, everyone would say that it was a cruel action. 28. But when they are silent about you, it amounts to a shout [of disapproval]. 29. But if you prefer to do a service to my praise and reputation, leave the city, betake yourself to your camp. 30. In training young men, violence must be avoided. 31. O that I may sometime be able to see that illustrious city, Rome!

Exercise 50.—1. Aliquā laetitiā et gaudiō perfruī in hāc vītā brevī nostrā omnēs cōnāmur. 2. Laus bona est sī ab aliīs et nōn ā nōbīs veniet. 3. Parentēs meī invītātī sunt ad urbem. 4. Praetōribus latrō-cinium impium rettulērunt. 5. Vīta hominum in mundō laetitiās ac dolōrēs habet. 6. Complūrēs voluptātēs brevēs quemdam dolōrem pariunt illīs quī eīs perfruantur. 7. Dextrīs manibus domō ējus in meā gladiōs trānstulērunt. 8. Sī latrōcinium impium brevī tempore relātum esset, cōnsul mīlitēs minimē trānstulisset. 9. Sī inimīcī meī armātī essent, gladium meum ā meā ipsīus dextrā manū ipsā raperent. 10. Solēbant deōs in templīs suīs cotidiē venerārī. 11. Voluntās adulēscēntis exercenda est. 12. Cicerō solēbat cotidiē sē exercere dīcendō. 13. Mīlitēs ad cīvēs concitandōs praemissī sunt. 14. Marīa māter Deī est; peperit Chrīstum quī Deus est. 15. Servus impius domō ējectus est.

Sight Translation, p. 284.—The Mother of the Gracchi, Part 2.

Cornelia was waiting at home for her son Tiberius, who was a tribune of the people and loved by the Roman people because he had for a long time desired to distribute land to the poor. "I wish my son would come home," Cornelia said to her friends and servants.

Just then a group of citizens is heard on the road. A servant said, "Your son is absent now, mistress."

Cornelia said, "Do you hear the shouting of the people and the voices of friends?"

Now they come before the eyes of the mother of the Gracchi. All remain silent, for they are bearing the body of Tiberius home. The tribune of the people had been killed by his enemies.

All were standing about. No one could speak. That admirable mother of the Gracchi at first said nothing. Finally she spoke as follows: "I have waited many hours now for my son. Today I love him and praise him especially, dead though he is, for he has proved himself valiant. For now I am the happiest of all women. My father overcame Hannibal. My husband brought back fame from Spain. I have given two sons to the state. Tiberius is here—having died for his fatherland. Gaius still lives; and for the fatherland he also will give all his strength. I am grateful to you, my friends, for having brought the body of my Tiberius back to me. Now I wish to give thanks to the immortal gods. Lead this woman to the shrine to the gods—daughter of Scipio, wife of Gracchus, mother of the Gracchi!"

The Roman people always praised this courageous woman. The citizens dedicated a monument to the excellent and courageous Cornelia with this short inscription, "The Mother of the Gracchi."

Answer in Latin, p. 285.—1. Whom was Cornelia awaiting at home? (Cornēlia domī fīlium Tiberium exspectābat.) 2. Tiberius was a tribune of the people, wasn't he? (Erat.) 3. Why was Tiberius loved by the Roman people? (Dīligēbātur quod agrōs pauperibus distribuere jam prīdem cupiēbat.) 4. What did Cornelia say to her friends and servants? ("Utinam," inquit Cornēlia, "domum veniat fīlius meus.") 5. Where was the shouting of the citizens heard? (Clāmor cīvium in viā audiēbātur.) 6. Why did all those who had come into Cornelia's home remain silent? (Tacēbant omnēs quod corpus Tiberiī portābant.) 7. By whom was Tiberius Gracchus killed? (Ab inimīcīs occīsus erat.) 8. What did the mother of Tiberius say at first? (Prīmō dīxit nihil.) 9. Afterwards what did she say? ("Ego sum," Cornēlia dīxit, "omnium mulierum beātissima, nam fīlius meus fortem sē ostendit.") 10. Why did Cornelia praise her son? (Eum laudāvit nam fortis erat.) 11. What did Cornelia say of her father? Of her husband? (Dīxit patrem Hannibalem superāvisse, virum suum glōriam sibi ex Hispaniā reportāvisse.) 12. What did she say of Gaius? (Dē Gājō dīxit eum prō patriā vivere et omnēs vīrēs datūrum esse.) 13. To whom did Cornelia express her gratitude? (Amīcīs grātiās ēgit.) 14. In what way did the Romans praise Cornelia? (Rōmānī Cornēliae monumentum dēdicāvērunt.) 15. What was the inscription on the monument? (Inscriptiō erat: "Māter Gracchōrum.") 16. What do you think of the mother of the Gracchi? (Putō eam mulierem optimam atque fortissimam fuisse.)

Lesson 13

Exercise 51.—1. Cicero plainly said that Catiline was not only the instigator of the evil, the originator of the conspiracy, but also the chief commander of the camp and most of all the leader of the enemy. (*Sceleris, conjūrātiōnis, castrōrum, hostium,* Gr. 681.) 2. On account of the bravery of a single leader all the soldiers replied that they would give their lives for the fatherland. (*Ūnīus ducis,* Gr. 683.) 3. Catiline had promised that he would set the city of Rome on fire. (*Urbem Rōmam,* Gr. 682.) 4. The bravest one of all the soldiers replied that not one of the enemy could hinder him. (*Ūnus ex mīlitibus omnium,* and *hostium,* Gr. 689.) 5. Men of this kind always burn with love of country. (*Patriae,* Gr. 684.) 6. If you hear anything new, listen carefully. (*Novī,* Gr. 693.) 7. Nearly the whole city of Rome was aflame. (*Urbs Rōma,* Gr. 682.) 8. At the arrival of Catiline all those of consular rank almost left the Senate. (*Catilīnae,* Gr. 683.) 9. After the slaves had been sent out of the city, the parents of the young men remained at Rome. (*Adulēscentium,* Gr. 680.) 10. But if I had sent the enemy against the town, they would have burned nearly all the buildings. 11. Did the expressions of the countenances of these senators move you not at all? (*Hōrum,* Gr. 680.) 12. We are not ignorant of what plans you made. (*Cōnsiliī,* Gr. 687.) 13. Which of us do you think is unaware of these facts? (*Nostrum,* Gr. 689.) 14. A state policy is not lacking. 15. There is still a little danger existing for me in that my enemy is living. (*Perīculī,* Gr. 693.)

16. Where in the world are we? (*Gentium*, Gr. 691.) 17. I have two swords. (*Mihi*, Gr. 725.) 18. The city of Rome was preserved by Cicero's diligence. (*Cicerōnis*, Gr. 683.) 19. What's new? Nothing new. (*Novī*, *novī*, Gr. 693.) 20. Praise brings forth its own hatred. (*Suī*, Gr. 683 or 684.) 21. The love of Christ impels us. (*Christī*, Gr. 684.) 22. We all ought to be moved rather by love of God than by fear. (*Deī*, Gr. 684.) 23. Catiline had decreed the death of all the leading men of the city. (*Principum*, Gr. 684.) 24. A majority of the citizens was held within the walls. (*Civium*, Gr. 686.) 25. All of us seem to have enough pain in this life. (*Nōs omnēs*, Gr. 694; *dolōris*, Gr. 690.) 26. The martyrs were men of great courage. (*Magnae fortitūdinis*, Gr. 691.) 27. Be of good mind. (*Bonō animō*, Gr. 698.) 28. All of these answered with one voice that they knew nothing new. (*Hī omnēs*, Gr. 694; *novī*, Gr. 693.) 29. The consul's home was in a near-by town. (*Cōnsulī*, Gr. 680.) 30. Would that I had more time for studying! (*Mihi*, Gr. 725; *temporis*, Gr. 687.)

Exercise 52.—1. Complūrēs hominēs vim vōcis lībertātis ignōrant. 2. Cōnsule auctōre, ex urbe Rōmā ēmissus est. 3. Metus perīculī mīlitem fortem numquam impedit. 4. Imperātor suōs in partem dexteram exercitūs mīsit. 5. Sīn autem nihil respondeat, dā eī satis temporis ad rem cogitandam. 6. Cīvēs bonī amōre patriae ārdent. 7. Sī cōnsul dīligenter nōn ēgisset, prope tōta urbs Rōma cōnflagrāta esset. 8. Omnēs prope Chrīstiānī antiquī sanguinem prō cāritāte Chrīste dēdērunt. 9. Adulēscens dīligenter respondit nihil novī esse. 10. Fortitūdō magna virtūs est, maximē mīlitum. 11. Timor Deī initium scientiae verae certē est. 12. Adhuc paulum perīculī est. 13. Domus Cicerōnis majōribus custōdibus mūnīta est. 14. In senātū nōn satis auctōritātis cōnsulī erat. 15. Ubinam gentium lībertās vera comperī potest? 16. Plūs novī quaesīvit. 17. Quid novī? Nihil novī. 18. Adventū Cicerōnis omnēs quī loquēbantur tacuērunt. 19. Timor mortis servōs impedīvit. 20. Hoc est tempus bonum loquendī dē reī pūblicae lēgibus. 21. Unus ex cōnsulibus dīxit nihil perīculī esse. 22. Deus omnibus nōbīs venerandus est. 23. Omnēs cīvēs cōnātī sunt eum appropinquantem impedīre. 24. Patientia incredibilis sānctīs erat. 25. Domus in urbe atque tectum in proximō oppidō parentibus meīs sunt. 26. Sanguis Chrīstī omnium animōrum nostrōrum pretium cārum est.

Exercise 53 [Ex Ōrātiōne contrā Praetōrēs Gallicōs Habita].— Etsī dīxerātis vōs velle servāre ac dēfendere salūtem omnium nostrum, tamen salūtī omnium Catholicōrum jam prīdem clam insidiābāminī. Omnibus vestrīs impetibus improbīs nostrā dīligentiā, auxiliō amīcōrum, grātiā Deī restitimus. Nunc vērō religiōnem universam, templa et tecta Galliae, fidem omnium Gallōrum apertē aggrediminī, eōrumque animās ipsās ad exitium et interitum dūcitis. Chrīstus nōn dīxit nōs in omnibus perīculīs victūrōs esse; hoc vērō dīxit, contrā ecclēsiam suam portās īnferī nōn praevalitūrās esse. Itaque in Deō omnis spēs nostra posita est.

From the Roman Missal, p. 290.—From the Ordinary of the Mass.

Accept, O holy Father, almighty and eternal God, this spotless host, which I, Thy unworthy servant, offer unto Thee, my living and true God, for my numberless sins, offenses, and failings, and for all here present; as also for all faithful Christians, both living and dead; that it may be profitable for my own and for their salvation unto life everlasting. Amen.

We offer unto Thee, O Lord, the chalice of salvation, beseeching Thy clemency that it may ascend in the sight of Thy divine Majesty with the odor of sweetness, for our salvation and for that of the whole world. Amen.

In a spirit of humility and with a contrite heart may we be accepted by Thee, O Lord, and may our sacrifice be so offered in Thy sight today that it may please Thee, O Lord God.

Lesson 14

Exercise 54.—1. Although the plots were disclosed, some nevertheless doubted. 2. If all the wicked were gathered into one place, this plague of the state would be restrained for a short time, yet not checked for all time. 3. The leader could not bring together his forces; for he was inexperienced in war. 4. We are not able to unite ourselves with our friends forever. 5. This was inscribed on the cross of Christ: Jesus of Nazareth, King of the Jews. 6. If Catiline had really been bound for Manlius' camp, he would have arrived without any delay. 7. If from so numerous a band of brigands only this one fellow is removed, it will perhaps seem for some short time that we have been liberated, but the danger will remain. 8. The leader sent one of the soldiers ahead to set the buildings on fire. 9. Your parents ought to act thus with you, and speak thus with you. 10. Not all of us can bear the thought of death with equanimity. 11. If my slaves feared me in the same way all the citizens fear you, I should think I ought to leave home. 12. Catiline thought his friend, that excellent Marcus Metellus, would be very solicitous in watching him, very courageous at punishing him. 13. For a long time I have scarcely been able to protect you from their armed assaults. 14. The citizens cannot safely remain within the same walls with men of this sort. 15. Young men of this sort are not far from prison. 16. The customs of my ancestors cannot deter me. 17. "Take up your cross," He says, "and follow Me." 18. "Without Me you can do nothing." 19. In that same year he became consul. 20. If I seek these things from God, should I not obtain them? 21. The noise of the speakers was heard. 22. But if they should fear the enemy, they would betake themselves from the walls for a short time. 23. Or do you fear the envy of your friends? 24. In the correction of young men parents ought never to be moved by hatred. 25. The authority of the state is most precious to all good men. 26. They sent the young man home in order to bring joy to his parents. 27. He summons armed men to inflict an impious war on the fatherland. 28. Not only the city of Rome but the whole of Italy had for a long time been subject to these perils and plots. 29. The injustices wrought by enemies are not always to be avenged. 30. Cicero understood that if this man had reached the Manlian camp, whither he was bound, there would be no one so stupid as not to see that a conspiracy had been formed nor anyone so deceitful as not to admit it openly.

Exercise 55.—1. In senātū sunt quī videantur īnsidiās inimīcōrum nōn intellegere. 2. Cicerō omnia oculīs populī patefierī voluit. 3. Sī nōn possumus in perpetuum hās īnsidiās comprimere, paulisper eās reprimāmus. 4. Omnēs mīlitēs in unum locum collectī sunt. 5. Sī cōnsul imperītus loquendī fuisset, mentēs cīvium inflammāre numquam potuisset. 6. Omnēs cīvēs oppidōrum in unum locum congregāvit et sē dūcem cum eīs conjunxit. 7. Sī haec verba in cruce nōn īnscrīpta essent, multī eōrum quī aderant nōn intellēxissent cūr Chrīstus ad mortem ductus esset. 8. Mīlēs domum contendēbat. 9. Nōn possumus vērē intellegere cūr jūra nostra sublāta sint.

From the Roman Missal, p. 295.—From the Canon of the Mass. O Lord Jesus Christ, who hast said to Thine apostles, Peace I leave you, My peace I give you: look not upon my sins, but upon the faith of Thy Church; and deign to give her peace and unity agreeably to Thy will: Who livest and reignest God, world without end. Amen.

O Lord Jesus Christ, Son of the living God, who, by the will of the Father and the cooperation of the Holy Spirit, hast by Thy death given life to the world: deliver me by this Thy most sacred body and blood from all my sinfulness and from all evil; and make me always cling to Thy commandments, and never permit me to be separated from Thee. Who with the same God the Father and the Holy Spirit, livest and reignest God, world without end. Amen.

Let not the partaking of Thy body, O Lord Jesus Christ, which I, though unworthy, presume to receive, turn to my judgment and condemnation; but by reason of Thy loving-kindness may it benefit me as a safeguard and an effective remedy, both of soul and of body. Who with God the Father, in the unity of the Holy Spirit, livest and reignest God, world without end. Amen.

Lesson 15

Exercise 56.—1. He himself came into the Senate in order more easily to explain the condition of things in a clear speech. (*Quō facilius expōneret*, Gr. 547.) 2. The praetors guarded all abodes in order that everyone could be made safe in the midst of the great peril and the plots of doom. (*Possent*, Gr. 546.) 3. The consul briefly explained the situation to the people in order to awaken dread of those who remained in the city. (*Ad cōnfirmandum timōrem*, Gr. 872.) 4. He said this to me in order to make it evident to me that the city of Rome had been founded by Romulus. (*Esset*, Gr. 546.) 5. After the founding of the city of Rome the Romans always preserved the laws in order that all the citizens might be safe. (*Possent*, Gr. 546.) 6. Soldiers ought to use every means to prevent beautiful homes from being consumed by fire. (*Cōnflagrentur*, Gr. 546.) 7. There are some who take no care at all. (*Prōvideant*, Gr. 634.) 8. St. Paul said many beautiful things in order to lead the souls of men to Christ. (*Dūceret*, Gr. 546.) 9. He sent several young men to aid the praetors. (*Auxiliō praetōribus*, Gr. 731.) 10. These beautiful sayings have been the means of salvation for some. (*Nōnnūllīs salūtī*, Gr. 731.) 11. Catiline departed from Rome in order to stir up war. (*Bellī excitandī causā*, Gr. 872.) 12. I sent two praetors to his abode to discover what the enemy of the state was contriving. (*Invenīrem*, Gr. 546.) 13. He asks his friend to await him a short time. (*Exspectet*, Gr. 546.) 14. He said this lest the fate of the wicked men be understood by the people. (*Intelligerētur*, Gr. 546.) 15. The praetor set out for his place of residence in order to carry out whatever weapons he might find. (*Efferret*, Gr. 546.) 16. The consul spoke a few words with us in order to avert this situation in the state. (*Ad hanc condiciōnem vitandam*, Gr. 872.) 17. The senators remained in the Senate for a short time to save themselves. (*Suī cōnservandī causā*, Gr. 877.) 18. Romulus was led by fate to Rome that he might found the city. (*Urbis condendae causā*, Gr. 872.) 19. The consul left guards outside the wall as a protection. (*Praesidiō*, Gr. 730.) 20. The death of our parents is always a great sorrow to us. (*Nōbīs magnō dolōrī*, Gr. 731.)

21. The hope of attaining eternal life is a joy to all Christians. (*Omnibus Christiānīs gaudiō*, Gr. 731.) 22. Death is not altogether sad. (*Dolōrī*, Gr. 730.) 23. Would that all friends were a strong help to us. (*Praesidiō*, Gr. 730.) 24. Are there not some who live to enjoy pleasure? (*Vīvant*, Gr. 633; *perfruantur*, Gr. 546.) 25. May God be to us a joy in life, a protection in death, salvation unto eternity. (*Gaudiō, praesidiō, salūtī*, Gr. 730.) 26. Because of the magnitude of the discovered crime, a few even in the Senate doubted the consul's words.

Exercise 57.—1. Paucīs verbīs breviter exposuit sē ad domicilium eōrum vēnisse ut ā metū ignis līberī essent. 2. Condiciōnibus pācis expositīs, cōnsul in castrīs trēs hōrās reī tantae magnitūdinis dēcernendae causā restitit. 3. Sī hic adulēscens dē fātō parentis nunc audīret, eī magnō dolōrī esset. 4. Praetor custōdem ad portās domiciliī pulchrī relīquit contrā ignem praesidiō. 5. Majōrēs quī rem pūblicam condidērunt lēgēs relīquērunt quibus jūra nostra custōdīrentur. 6. Omnia quae poterat ēgit ut manus nefāriōrum improba ā manibus fātī ēriperētur. 7. Eī quī patriam suam relīquērunt urbis nostrae condendae causā hominēs magnī animī (magnanimī) erant. 8. Manifestum est Deum Fīlium suum nōbīs salūtī mīsisse. 9. Urbs pulchra Rōma multīs annīs ante tempus Chrīstī condita est. 10. Haec victōria nōbīs magnō gaudiō, hostibus autem dolōrī est. 11. Parentēs carōs videndī causā veniet. 12. Domicilium pulchrum eīs Rōmae est. 13. Sī eī (in eum, *ecclesiastical Latin*) crēdimus, Deus prōvidēbit. 14. Sī rēs pūblica hōs cīvēs honestōs in exilium mīserit, illī urbem novam in quā incolant condent. 15. Dominus sit mihi in hāc vītā praesidiō et in vītā quae post mortem veniet salūtī. 16. Populīs omnem rem exposuit nē quis ignōrāret quid agerētur. 17. Chrīstus apertē locūtus est ut ab invidiā eōrum quī eum oderant salvus esset. 18. Haec dīcō nē quis arbitrētur mē invidiam metuere.

Exercise 58.—Model: And so yesterday I called to my side Lucius Flaccus and Gaius Pomptinus, the praetors, very courageous and patriotic men; I explained the situation and showed them what ought to be done.

1. Itaque duābus post hōrīs Lentulum et Cethēgum, nefārissimōs et perditissimōs virōs, cēpit, Rōmam mīsit, in vincula conjēcit.

2. Itaque Corinthum, pulchram et illustrem urbem, terrā marīque obsēdit, quīntō diē cēpit, decem diēs tecta, domicilia, templa incendit.

3. Itaque ipsā nocte īnfantem Jesum et Marīam, mātrem sānctissimam ējus, accēpit, in Aegyptum fūgit, ibi multōs annōs habitāvit.

4. Itaque abhinc quīnque annōs et Cicerōnem et Hortensium, ora-

tōrēs illustrēs, in forō loquentēs audīvit, eōs laudāvit, postulāvit ut in dīcendō in senātū sē exercerent.

Exercise 59.—"Cum cognōvissem inimīcissimum reī pūblicae in urbe adesse, Wellington et Reynolds, duōs praetōrēs fidēlēs, ad mē vocāvī; rem eīs exposuī; quid fierī placēret ostendī. Eōs mīsī quī vidērent num vērē esset is quem quaerēbāmus, et quid ageret aut mōlīrētur. Eōs jussī omnia comperīre ut facinora istīus manifestissima essent nōn modo sibi ipsīs sed et jūdicibus.

"Hī duo virī fortissimī nōn modo negōtium sine morā et sine recūsātiōne suscēpērunt, sed virum ipsum eōdem illō diē cēpērunt et in vincula conjēcērunt."

Lesson 16

Exercise 60.—1. What was the king to do? (*Faceret*, Gr. 510.) 2. In such an extraordinary political crisis what shall I say? (*Dicam*, Gr. 510.) 3. Should I not put this man to death? (*Dūcam*, Gr. 510.) 4. Granted that he was not a big man, yet he was to be feared by me. (*Fuerit*, Gr. 519.) 5. Was I not to make use of his services? (*Ūterer*, Gr. 510.) 6. He may be well known; he may be famous; he is not an honorable man. (*Sit, sit*, Gr. 519.) 7. What was the consul to hope for but death? (*Optāret*, Gr. 510.) 8. Let the crowds come; fear of the people moves me not at all. (*Veniant*, Gr. 519.) 9. Next he came to stir up the wicked citizens. 10. He was surprised, however, in the very act of stirring up these citizens. 11. What are we to offer to God, who has given us so many good things? (*Offerāmus*, Gr. 510.) 12. Let him carry the order to the consul; this will be satisfactory to me. (*Dēferat*, Gr. 519.) 13. Who will deny this? (*Neget*, Gr. 510.) 14. Suppose it is not true! What then? (*Fuerit*, Gr. 519.) 15. I grant they are brave, but I don't fear them. (*Sint*, Gr. 519.) 16. Whither will they go? (*Cōnferent*, Gr. 489.) 17. How long were they to remain in the city? (*Manēret*, Gr. 510.) 18. Was I to hand over a sword to this pest? (*Trāderem*, Gr. 510.) 19. Granted the orders are difficult, they are nevertheless not to be violated. (*Sint*, Gr. 519.) 20. Thereupon the crowds sought the praetor's assistance in order to catch the one known to be an enemy. 21. If all these facts had been brought to the leading men of the state, the enemy's plots would have been thwarted. 22. All the well-known citizens offered their services to the consuls. 23. If you had judged Catiline worthy of death, would you have allowed him even one hour to live? 24. When he had said this, Cicero finally became silent. (*Haec locūtus*, Gr. 914.) 25. When he had said this, the conspiracy was seen to be found out. (*Hīs dictīs*, Gr. 914.) 26. The Manlian camp was not at Rome but it was in Italy. (*Rōmae*, Gr. 915.) 27. All those who had gone into exile have returned to their fatherland, Rome. 28. I know not why the consul dared speak of domestic disgrace, for he was doing harm to the reputation of a private citizen.

Exercise 61.—1. Nē frequentēs vēnerint, opera nostra nōn omninō frūstrā oblāta est. 2. Sit vērum, nēmō crēdet eum hoc mandātum dēdisse. 3. Cui hanc rem gravem referrem? 4. Quid deinde dīceret? 5. Propter operam ējus poteram impetrāre id quod jam dūdum optābam. 6. Quō mīlitēs fugientēs sē conferrent? 7. Quid praetor dē hōc mandātō dīceret? 8. Propter dīligentiam cōnsulis et operam praetōris imperātor nōtus sollicitāre cīvēs nōn poterat. 9. Quid cōnsul senātuī frequentī dīceret? 10. Hostis reī pūblicae in ipsīs cīvibus sollicitandīs dēprehensus est. 11. Ego jam prīdem optābam mē operamque meam cīvitātī offerre. 12. Senātor nōtus domī suae dēprehensus est. Jam dūdum mandāta cīvitātis hostibus clam dēferēbat. 13. Deinde facultās quam jam dūdum optābat Cicerōnī oblāta est. 14. Quōmodō servī omnēs gladiōs domō meā dēferrent? 15. Sit bonus; tamen jūra cīvium violāvit.

Exercise 62.—In multīs et maximīs perīculīs versābāmur. In Italiā erant castra virōrum nefāriōrum ac perditōrum quī urbem incendere et cīvēs interficere voluērunt (cōgitārent, *if treated as characteristic clause*). Etiam Rōmae erant hostēs; immō imperātor et dux hostium erat in urbe, in quem adeō cupiēbat bellum impium inferre. In senātū ipsō conjūrātōs vīdī, quōs coāctus sum rogāre quid dē rē pūblicā sentīrent. Et, quod maximē timendum erat, hī nōn dubitāvērunt legiōnibus nostrīs bellī inferrendī causā Gallōs sollicitāre.

Quid facerēmus? Quō nōs verterēmus? Quae mandāta darentur? Quōrum opera adhibērētur? Deinde facultās mihi oblāta est, quam semper obtābam. Hostēs reī pūblicae deprehensī sunt; ego urbem cōnservāvī; metū cīvēs līberāvī; ā peste ac perniciē domicilia cīvium et templa deōrum ēripuī.

Fuerit Catilīna cīvis; fuerint conjūrātī Rōmānī; quis est quī mē propter dīligentiam in cīvitāte cōnservandā nōn laudet?

Exercise 63.—1. Corinthum, urbem pulchram nōtamque, terrā marīque obsēdit. 2. Hanc urbem nōtam cōnservāvī. 3. Virōs praemīsī quī Gallōs caperent. 4. Exposuī quid fierī placēret. 5. Eōs in carcerem dūxit. 6. Dūcem hostium interficī jussērunt. 7. Explōrātōrēs mīsī quī comperīrent quid hostēs agerent. 8. Istum mīsī quī tēla comparāret. 9. Dīxit sē amīcum meum semper fuisse. 10. Ēgredere ex urbe. 11. Mē interficere jam diū cōnāris. 12. Quid dīcat quisquam? 13. Dīxī ego īdem

tē omnēs nōs interficere cōnātūrum esse. 14. Utinam Cicerō, vir fortis-
simus, vīveret. 15. Veniat! 16. Nē id dīxerīs. 17. Mūtā jam istam
mentem. 18. Sī exeat, urbs perīculō līberārētur. 19. Lībera mē metū.
20. Sit fortis. 21. Num hoc dīcere audēs? 22. Cūr in senātum vēnit?
23. Sī parentēs tē ōdissent, quid facerēs? 24. Sī Rōma vastata esset, nōs
Cicerōnem nōn legerēmus. 25. Sī quid Catilīna agat scīs, cūr eum in
vincula nōn conjicīs? 26. Sī domum tua vēnerit, eum interficere nē
dubitāverīs. 27. Quis mīlitēs reprehendat? 28. Quid Cicero faceret?
29. Sīc jam agam nōn ut timōre sed ut amōre patriae mōtus. 30. Sī
omnēs improbī in carcere essent, metū līberī essemus. 31. Dīxit sē
Rōmā ēgressūrum esse. 32. In Galliā erat defectiō. 33. Per prōvinciam
iter fēcērunt. 34. Rōmae erant complūrēs perditī.

Lesson 17

Exercise 64.—1. At Rome the consuls were men of unlimited power.
(*Īnfīnītā potestāte,* Gr. 762.) 2. Very clear proofs were brought forward by the praetor. (*Ā praetōre,* Gr. 764.) 3. In the state someone is
always ambitious for power. (*Potestātis,* Gr. 723.) 4. I think that the
evidence should be read aloud to the Senate by the consul. (*Ā cōnsule,*
Gr. 764, 882.) 5. He took care to fortify the city by means of walls.
(*Moenibus,* Gr. 765.) 6. Many citizens were born in a humble state.
(*Obscūrō locō,* Gr. 915.) 7. The consul read the letters aloud with great
care. (*Magnā dīligentiā,* Gr. 769.) 8. I admit that men differ among
themselves in their customs. (*Mōribus,* Gr. 770.) 9. The other consul
spoke a little longer. (*Paulō,* Gr. 771.) 10. My friend is very fond of
reading. (*Legendī,* Gr. 723.) 11. He often pointed out that parents are
loved by their children. (*Ā suīs līberīs,* Gr. 764.) 12. Even if this consul
is not eager for power, yet he is worthy of some power. (*Aliquā potestāte,* Gr. 776.) 13. There are some who think that power is dearer
than life. (*Vītā,* Gr. 777.) 14. God Himself has made everything that
we see with almighty power and yet there are some that do not love
Him. (*Īnfīnītā potestāte,* Gr. 769.)

Exercise 65.—1. Indicium ā cōnsule in senātum introductum erat.
2. Cēnsuit sē potestāte suā īnfīnītā ūtī oportēre. 3. Semper legendī
studiōsus sum. 4. Sī litterae ā cōnsulibus nōn recitatae essent, nemō
indicium confessus esset. 5. Cūret cōnsul nē aliquis in senātū īnfīnītae
potestātis studiōsus sit. 6. Sī aliquod indicium introductum erit, virōs
quī litteras recitāverint, indicāre poterimus. 7. Sī parentēs amāverīs, tē
amābunt. 8. Multī sunt quī studiōsī litterās accipiendī sint, paucī autem
eās scrībendī. 9. Ā praetōre aliquid indicābātur. 10. Cethegus paulō ante

dīxerat aliquid dē glādiīs quī domō suā erant elātī. 11. Litterīs vērō recitātīs, īnsidiās confessus est. 12. Censuērunt urbem igne vastandam [esse]. 13. Caesar vir īnfīnītā potestāte et summā auctoritāte factus est; interfectus autem est vī et manibus amīcōrum. 14. Inter nōs mōribus differimus. 15. Lībera metū rem pūblicam. 16. Catilīna parentibus clarīs natus est. 17. Dūx confessus est sē eā potestāte quae ā senātū eī data erat nōn contentus esse. 18. Censeō multō plūra virtūte quam potestāte efficī posse. 19. Maximā cum dīligentiā vītās et lībertātem omnium cīvium custōdīvī. 20. Catilīna vir maximā audāciā erat. 21. Multīs et magnīs perīculīs rēs pūblica līberāta est.

Exercise 66.—1. The state has been saved by the planning and care of Cicero. (*Cōnsiliō* and *dīligentiā*, Gr. 765.) 2. Every noble man hears with pleasure the praise of others. (*Cum gaudiō*, Gr. 769.) 3. We have hurled down your swords from you. (*Ā vōbīs*, Gr. 766.) 4. Their plans have been discovered by my efforts. (*Per mē*, Gr. 975.) 5. I will explain to you by what means they were discovered. (*Quā ratiōne*, Gr. 765.) 6. Up to this time they are with us. (*Nōbīscum*, Gr. 772.) 7. Now we see the crime with our own eyes. (*Oculīs*, Gr. 765.) 8. The Gauls were stirred up by Lentulus. (*Ā Lentulō*, Gr. 764.) 9. The envoys arrived with a considerable retinue. (*Magnō comitātū*, Gr. 773.) 10. Swords are unsheathed by our men. (*Ā nostrīs*, Gr. 764.) 11. The dispatch has not been opened by me. (*Ā mē*, Gr. 764.) 12. Cicero and Catiline differ greatly from one another in point of virtue. (*Virtūte*, Gr. 770.) 13. You've got everybody outdone in effrontery. (*Audāciā*, Gr. 770.) 14. He ordered him to come as soon as possible with his army. (*Cum exercitū*, Gr. 772.) 15. He determined to join these men. (*Cum hīs*, Gr. 772.) 16. He had an argument with the others. (*Cum cēterīs*, Gr. 772.) 17. They had been written in his own hand. (*Manū*, Gr. 765.) 18. But this power did not deter you from your heinous crime. (*Ā maximō scelere*, Gr. 932.) 19. He did this impelled by fear. (*Timōre*, Gr. 765.) 20. He excelled all others in his skill at speaking. (*Scientiā*, Gr. 770; *dīcendī*, Gr. 684.) 21. The Romans were great-souled men. (*Magnī animī*, Gr. 762.) 22. The state has been freed from terrible dangers. (*Maximīs perīculīs*, Gr. 766.) 23. These things I foresaw. (*Animō*, Gr. 765 or 770.) 24. All these things have unquestionably been carried on by the will of the immortal gods. 25. He was a man of great reputation. (*Magnī nōminis*, Gr. 762.) 26. Was Cicero a man of large physique? (*Magnō corpore*, Gr. 762.) 27. I must live with those whom I have conquered. (*Cum eīs*, Gr. 772.) 28. I have defended the city by means of guards and night watches. (*Custōdiīs vigiliīsque*,

Gr. 765.) 29. I will try with all my strength. (*Omnibus viribus*, Gr. 769.) 30. No one was fonder of speaking than Cicero. (*Cicerōne*, Gr. 777.)

Exercise 67.—1. Est nōtum quidem signum. 2. Cūrā ut vir sīs. 3. Litterae erant in hanc sententiam. 4. Vehementissimē permōtus. . . . 5. Ac nē longum sit. . . . 6. Imāgō avī tuī est. 7. Surrēxit. 8. Ac nē longum sit. . . . 9. Litterae ipsīus manū scrīptae. . . . 10. Hae litterae erant in eandem ferē sententiam. 11. Ac nē longum sit. . . . 12. Litterae sine nōmine erant. 13. Cūrā ut vir sīs. 14. Scelere dēmēns. . . . 15. Esto fortī animō. 16. Tē ā tantō scelere revocāre dēbuit. 17. Vehementissimē permōtus. . . . 18. Bonōrum ferramentōrum studiōsus. . . . 19. Ac nē longum sit. . . . 20. Dīxit in eandem ferē sententiam. 21. Amantissimus reī pūblicae erat. 22. Prīmum ille dīxit "Ita." 23. Quaesīvit ab illīs quid sibi esset cum eīs. 24. Dīcendī ējus exercitātiō defēcit. 25. Breviter constanterque respondit. 26. Litterae sine nomine sunt. 27. Ad extremum nihil ex eīs quae Gallī īnsimulābant negāvit. 28. Nōnnumquam inter sē aspiciēbant. 29. Senātus hās acerrimās ac fortissimās sententiās sine ūllā varietāte est secūtus. 30. Consultum senātūs ex memōriā vōbīs exponam. 31. Ac nē longum sit. . . . 32. Quis sim, sciēs ex eō quem ad tē mīsī. 33. Bonōrum telōrum studiōsus erat.

Exercise 68 [Quī Patriam Tradidit Condemnātur].—Alterum intrōdūxī quī vehementissimē perturbārī vidēbātur. Cui litterās ostendimus quās praetōrēs ē domiciliō ējus paulō ante extulerant. Sine nōmine erant. Atque ille prīmō quidem negāvit eās ā sē esse scrīptās, sed tandem, indiciō perturbātus, confessus est sē litterās scrīpsisse. Exclāmāvit vērō sē timōre inductum eās scrīpsisse, sē amantissimum reī pūblicae esse, sē rem pūblicam cīvēsque extinguere mōluisse. Cūjus facinus vērō tantum erat ut praetōrēs misericordiā nōn movērentur. Eum statim interficī jussērunt.

Cicero's Sense of Humor, p. 310.—But I am amazed that you all disregard Cicero's jests, in which he was ever ready, as in all things. Cicero was once dining at Damasippus' house and the host, putting forth some second-rate wine, said, "Try this Falernian; it's forty years old." "Indeed," said Cicero, "it doesn't show its age at all."

Again, when he saw his son-in-law Lentulus, a man of small build, girded with a long sword, he said, "Who tied my son-in-law to the sword?"

Nor did he spare his brother Quintus Cicero, for once when he saw in the province which the latter ruled a picture of him—head and shoulders only, as was the custom, painted in bold strokes, he said (for

Quintus himself was of small build), "This half of my brother is larger than the whole of him."

Cicero said to Curius, who lied a great deal about the years of his age: "Then when we were practising speaking in public together, you were not yet born." Again, when Fabia said she was thirty years old, he said, "It must be true. I've been hearing her say it now for twenty years."

Lesson 18

Exercise 69.—1. We should so face all dangers as to overcome them. (*Ut vincāmus*, Gr. 550.) 2. The enemy were not the kind that could be driven away easily. (*Qui dēpellerentur*, Gr. 550.) 3. The witnesses were so terrified that they could not speak openly. (*Ut nōn possent*, Gr. 550.) 4. It is certain that this crime is such that it may be rightly and justly punished. (*Ut pūniātur*, Gr. 550.) 5. No peril is so extreme but that it can be borne well. (*Quin possit*, Gr. 552.) 6. He was so well fitted for public speaking that he has now become consul. (*Ut sit*, Gr. 550.) 7. It was fortunate that the praetors went to meet them. (*Quod occurrerunt*, Gr. 659.) 8. It was fortunate that the witnesses gave themselves into custody. (*Quod dedērunt*, Gr. 659.) 9. Nothing prevents the publication of this letter. (*Quōminus ēdantur*, Gr. 646.) 10. First let us prevent the enemy from routing our men. (*Quōminus dēpellant*, Gr. 646.) 11. We will prevent him from punishing the witnesses now. (*Nē pūniat*, Gr. 645.) 12. The fact that he went out still alive is more to be feared. (*Quod exiit*, Gr. 658.) 13. It was fortunate that I saw you. (*Quod vīdī*, Gr. 659.) 14. It is certain that they will be with us. 15. I exhorted him to explain everything without fear. 16. The witness openly stated that he had a letter addressed to Catiline. 17. He prayed that they do everything that they had promised. 18. He replied that he had always been a collector of good pictures. 19. The slaves were not fitted to undergo the danger. 20. He discovered that it was all true. 21. The darts were so flung that it seemed they could not be avoided. (*Vidērentur*, Gr. 550.) 22. So boldly did our soldiers advance that the enemy fled. (*Fugerent*, Gr. 550.) 23. He lived so well that to remember his friends was a great joy. (*Ut sit*, Gr. 550.) 24. He praised them for loving God. 25. Christ rose on the third day as He said.

Exercise 70.—1. Bene accidit quod testis nōn mortuus est. 2. Quod aptus sum ad hās difficultātēs obeundās tuum est. 3. Testēs adeō metuērunt ut palam loquī nōn possent. 4. Cīvēs adeō pūnītī sunt ut ā patriā dēpellerentur. 5. Facinus tantum erat ut testēs dē eō legere nōn possent. 6. Prīmum praetōrī occurrit. Deinde cōnātus est obstāre quōminus ille palam loquerētur. 7. Constat amīcōs Catilīnae prohibitūrōs esse quōminus cōnsul eum dēpellat. 8. Mēns ējus apta erat ad morēs populī intellegendōs. 9. Sī Catilīna patriae īnsidiātus est, meritō et jūre pūniendus est. 10. Constat hōs adulēscentēs nōn modo aptōs exercituī esse.

Exercise 71.—1. Tam fortiter pugnāvērunt ut hostēs vincerent (vīcerint). 2. Cicerō rem pūblicam tam fortiter dēfendit ut eum omnēs nunc laudēmus. 3. Erant talēs quī contrā rem pūblicam conjūrārent. 4. Invidia ējus erat tanta ut Rōmā exīret (exierit). 5. Scelera ējus tot et tanta erant ut senātus eum statim condemnāret (condemnāverit). 6. Testēs tot erant ut omnia tandem cōnfiterētur (cōnfessus sit). 7. Utinam sīc vītam ēgisset ut nōs eum laudāre possēmus. 8. Utinam sīc dīxisses ut tibi credere possēmus. 9. Scelera ējus tam manifesta erant ut nemō eum dēfenderet (dēfenderint). 10. Cicerō tam dīligēns erat ut rēs pūblica perīculīs līberārētur (līberāta sit). 11. Adeō fortiter pugnāvērunt ut Cicerō eōs laudāret (laudāverit). 12. Catilīna tam audax erat ut ipse Cicerō sum timēret. 13. Tanta erat celeritās ējus ut hostēs eī īnsidiārī nōn possent. 14. Ita sē gessit in rē pūblicā ut manifestum esset facta ējus nōn cāsū sed virtūte gesta esse. [The alternate forms given are perfect in secondary sequence to emphasize actual occurrence; Gr. 554.]

Exercise 72.—Model: He alone of all those men was to be feared, but only so long as he was within the walls of the city.

1. Peccātum est ūnum timendum omnibus vōbīs, sed tam diū dum in hōc urbe terrārum versāminī.

2. Deus est dīligendus plūsquam omnia alia, sed ita ut hominēs eōdem amōre dīligātis.

3. Lībertās est maximā dīligentiā dēfendenda, sed ita ut lēgēs et pax etiam serventur.

Exercise 73.—1. Rēs pūblica perīculīs līberāta est. 2. Perīculīs līberātī sumus. 3. Ā Cicerōne līberatī sumus. 4. Gallus ā Rōmānīs captus est. 5. Omnēs scientiā dīcendī superābat. 6. Dūcēs cum Gallīs īvērunt. 7. Dīligentiā et cōnsiliō rem pūblicam servāvit. 8. Dīligentiā et virtūte Cicerōnis vītae nostrae servātae sunt. 9. Caesar scientiā pugnandī omnēs superābat. 10. Homō magnae virtūtis erat. 11. Litterae sine nōmine erant. 12. Erat eī mēns ad facinus apta. 13. Deōrum nūtū servātī sumus. 14. Per Gallum litterās mīsimus. 15. Ante lūcem venīre voluērunt. 16. Magnā cum dīligentiā lībertās nōbīs dēfendenda est. 17. Haec, illō absente, gesta sunt. 18. Aliīs praesentibus, dē rē loquī noluit. 19. Ille erat ūnus timendus ex istīs omnibus. 20. Sī in urbe mansisset, nōs in perīculō adhūc versārēmur. 21. Utinam ēfūgissem. 22. Utinam istās litterās nē scrīpsissēs. 23. Rēs pūblica conservētur. 24. Per Gallōs īnsidiās cognōvit. 25. Per Gallōs litterās mittunt.

Exercise 74.—1. Erat eī mēns ad facinus apta. 2. Ut levissimē dīcam. . . . 3. Ille erat ūnus timendus. 4. Tantā pāce, tantō otiō, tantō silentiō. . . . 5. Ut levissimē dīcem. . . . 6. Cōnsiliō neque lingua neque manus deerat 7. Dīligēns in rēbus perditīs erat. 8. Tantō ante diem. . . . 9. Exitiī ac fatī diēs. . . . 10. Nihil erat quod nōn ipse obīret. 11. Omnium aditūs tenēbat. 12. Poterat, audēbat. 13. Ad certās rēs conficiendās certōs hominēs delectōs ac descriptōs habēbat. 14. Dīcam id quod sentiō. 15. Manifestō dēprehensus. . . . 16. Dīmicandum nōbīs cum illō fuisset.

From the Roman Missal, p. 317.—From the Ordinary of the Mass. In the beginning was the Word, and the Word was with God, and the Word was God. He was in the beginning with God. All things were made through Him, and without Him was made nothing that has been made. In Him was life, and the life was the light of men: and the light shines in the darkness, and the darkness grasped it not. There was a man, one sent from God, whose name was John. This man came as a witness, to give proof concerning the Light, that all might believe through Him. He was not himself the Light, but he was to bear witness to the Light. It was the true Light that enlightens every man who comes into this world. He was in the world, and the world was made by Him, and the world knew Him not. He came unto His own, and His own received Him not. But to as many as received Him, He gave the power of becoming sons of God, to those who believe in His Name. Who were born not of blood, nor of the will of the flesh, nor of the will of man, but of God. AND THE WORD WAS MADE FLESH, and dwelt among us; and we saw His glory, the glory as of the only-begotten of the Father, full of grace and truth. Thanks be to God.

Lesson 19

Exercise 75.—1. The memorial in this city is not so great as I had heard. 2. It is the leader's place to commond; the soldier's, to obey. 3. All that I have told you is as true as it is extraordinary. 4. It is a father's duty to train his children in virtue. 5. There are not as many present in the Senate as the consul summoned. 6. It is a witness's duty to speak the truth. 7. The citizens did not wish to hear always the same thing. 8. It is our duty to serve God. 9. The louder you speak, the better you can be heard. 10. But after this Joseph of Arimathea asked of Pilate that he might take the body of Jesus, and Pilate permitted it. So Joseph came and took the body. 11. There was in that place a new tomb in which no one had ever been buried. There they laid Jesus therefore. 12. But the witnesses were not willing to tell the truth. 13. The consul himself carried on an unprovoked war with foreign tribes but imperfectly subjugated. 14. Then turning toward the people, he exhorted them to hear the truth. 15. I did not wish to reply badly; I was unwilling to speak unasked. 16. The consul must see to it that the state suffers no harm. 17. As often as the consul escaped from his hands, just so often did Catiline make an attempt on his life. 18. Catiline was not the same sort of man as Cicero. 19. The witness replied just as I myself would have replied.

Exercise 76.—1. Omnia cōnsilia tua nōbīs clāriōra lūce sunt. 2. Glōria mihi cārior est vītā ipsa. 3. Hīc est idem quem Rōmae vīdimus. 4. Eōrum nōn causam quaerere; eōrum nōn respondēre, eōrum modō agere ac morī. 5. Est nostrum dē salūte et corporis et animae prōvidēre. 6. Nōn voluit sīc agere ut eī imperāveram (agere perinde ac jusseram). 7. Quō plūs loquēbātur, eō minus attendēbant. 8. Testis bonī est vēra loquī. 9. Monumentum nōn tam pulchrum erat quam arbitrātus sum. 10. Exercitus nōn tantus erat quantum arbitrātus erat. 11. Tālis es, quālis fuistī semper. 12. In senātū tot sententiae erant quot erant hominēs. 13. Tam dīligēns est quam fortis. 14. Idem ēgit quod ēgissēs. 15. Cōnsulis est dē salūte reī pūblicae prōvidēre. 16. Monumentum quod statuerant mājus erat quam arbitrātus essēs. 17. Sīcut Caesar maximus imperator Rōmānus erat, ita Cicerō maximus ōrātor Rōmānus erat. 18. Mīlitēs aliēnī tam barbarī erant quam fortēs. 19. Imperātor ad mīlitēs ējus sē convertit et idem dīxit quod paulō anteā dīxerat. 20. Hī aliēnī male loquuntur. 21. Quō celerius ex hōc locō discesseris, eō melius. 22. Sunt aliēnī quī ultrō bellum gerant. 23. Accidit perinde ac Cicerō praevīderat.

Exercise 77.—1. Est quidem nōtum signum. 2. Cūrā ut vir sīs (Estō fortis). 3. Litterae sine nōmine erant. 4. Ut levissimē dīcam. 5. Erat dīligēns in perditīs rēbus. 6. Ā Cicerōne servātī sumus. 7. Mē hīs perīculīs līberā. 8. Vir erat vehementissimē perturbātus. 9. Litterae sine nōmine erant. 10. Ipsīus manū scrīptae sunt. 11. Signum cognōvit. 12. Utinam profūgissem. 13. Eōs laudāvit quod senātum dēfendissent. 14. Grātiae Deō ā nōbīs habendae sunt. 15. Omnēs amīcōs suōs scientiā dīcendī superāvit. 16. Gallia ā Caesare pācāta est. 17. Vestrum est mē dēfendere. 18. Bonī mīlitis est rem pūblicam dēfendere. 19. Prōvidēbō ut omnēs in perpetuā pāce esse possītis. 20. Utinam nē Caesar Gallōs pācāvisset. 21. Dīxit hostēs venīre. 22. Abhinc quīnque annōs hunc Rōmae vīdimus. 23. Negāvit sē Rōmam umquam ventūrum esse. 24. Accidit ut hostibus in silvīs occurrerent. 25. Eādem nocte accidit ut lūna esset plēna. 26. Quis mē jūre reprehendat? 27. Rogāvit mē ut eōs adjuvārem. 28. Bene accidit quod nōn interfectus es. 29. Hūc urbis videndae causā vēnit. 30. Sī Rōmae essēs, papam vidērēs. 31. Caesar sī vīveret dux maximus esset. 32. Trībus diēbus ad montēs perveniēmus. 33. Ex urbe ēgrediātur. 34. Sī Deum timēmus, cūr hominēs timeāmus? 35. Ēgērunt quasi odiō movērentur. 36. Nolī illum interficere. 37. Duābus post hōrīs Lentulus captus est. 38. Inimicīssimus reī pūblicae captus est. 39. Negōtium sine morā suscēpērunt. 40. Virōs eō misī quī inimīcōs caperent. 41. Repente omnia confessus est. 42. In eandem sententiam locutus est. 43. Surrēxit. 44. Imāgō avī ējus erat. 45. Eāsdem litterās eī ostendimus quae ex domō ējus delatae erant. 46. Cum in senātum paulō ante vēnistī, quis ex omnibus hīs hominibus tē vīdit?

Exercise 78.—1. Omnis hīc orbis terrārum nūtū et potestāte dīvīnā administrātur. 2. Quōs ego sī mē compressisse dīcam, nimium mihi sumam. 3. Est enim in mē is animus. 4. Magnum enim est in bonīs praesidium. 5. Nōn video quidquam altius quō mihi libeat ascendere. 6. Nōn essem ferendus. . . . 7. Cīvitās malē pācāta. . . . 8. Bellum facere possunt et nōn nolunt. 9. Nullum ego praemium postulō praeterquam hūjus dieī memōriam sempiternam. 10. Et urbem et cīvēs integrōs incolumēsque servāvit. 11. Sine caede. . . . 12. Lumina cīvitātis exstīncta sunt. 13. Post hominum memōriam. . . .

Exercise 79.—1. Litterae sine nōmine erant. 2. Ut levissimē dīcam, maximīs perīculīs servātī sumus. 3. Scientiā dīcendī omnēs Rōmānōs superābat. 4. Negāvit sē litterās scrīpsisse. 5. Utinam istās litterās nē cēpissēs. 6. Imaginem patris suī cognōvit. 7. Rōmam quam celerrimē īvit. 8. Erat eī mens ad facinus apta. 9. Eōs laudāvit quod fortiter pugnāvissent. 10. Quae cum ita sint, eōs laudēmus. 11. Acerbissimō suppliciō dignī sunt. 12. Tandem, nē longum sit, omnēs eōs ad mortem dūximus. 13. Signa sua cognōvērunt. 14. Litterae ipsīus manū scrīptae sunt. 15. Omnis hīc orbis terrārum quem vidēmus potestāte dīvīnā administrātur. 16. Jam diū contrā vītās omnium nostrum machināris. 17. Patent portae; proficīscere! 18. Virōs praemīsit quī castra caperent. 19. Bene contingat. 20. Sānctī vērī est Deum praeter omnia dīligere.

Exercise 80.—In rēbus adversīs, cīvēs Americānī, versātī sumus; rēs pūblica maximīs perīculīs tandem servāta est. Patria nostra in perīculō fuit nōn sōlum propter cīvium īnsidiās et dissensiōnēs sed etiam propter bella aliēna atque impetūs inimīcārum gentium. Num quisquam īnfitiārī potest nōs ex omnibus hīs perīculīs servātōs esse nōn sōlum operā et studiō cōnsulum sed etiam nūtū ac potestāte Deī, quī lībertātem et salūtem bonōrum dēfendit? Itaque grātiae Deō ā nōbīs certissimē habendae sunt, quia ab eō ēreptī sumus gladiō, igne, interitū ipsō.

Lesson 20

Exercise 81.—1. Although the defendant denied the accusation, the judges convicted him of robbery. (*Quamquam negāvit,* Gr. 595.) 2. Although nothing had made him worthy of death, the young man was sentenced to death. (*Quamquam fēcerat,* Gr. 595.) 3. However honorable the witnesses may have been, the judge did not believe their testimony. (*Quamvīs essent,* Gr. 596.) 4. Even if witnesses had not been present, the accused man would nevertheless have been condemned because of his dishonor. (*Etiamsī adessent,* Gr. 598.) 5. Although the judge may be very fond of eloquence, he speaks badly. (*Licet sit,* Gr. 597.) 6. Granted that the strength is not present, nevertheless the will is praiseworthy. (*Ut adsint,* Gr. 596.) 7. The more he was accused of wickedness the more he denied it. (*Nēquitiae,* Gr. 717.) 8. Although it is easy to accuse foreign nations of waging war, nevertheless we should not be in a hurry to condemn them all. (*Quamvīs sit,* Gr. 596; *bellī,* Gr. 717.) 9. The crime was so dreadful that no eloquence could save the accused man. 10. Although he could have denied the crime, he suddenly confessed. (*Cum posset,* Gr. 596.) 11. Although Cicero saw that his own destruction was linked with the state's terrible misfortune, he nevertheless did not avoid personal danger. (*Quamquam vidēbat,* Gr. 595.) 12. This disgrace, although unbearable, he nevertheless bore as well as he could. (*Quamquam fuit,* Gr. 595.)

Exercise 82.—1. Quamquam crīminis incredibilis accūsor, jūdicēs, tamen meritō et jūre mē capite damnāre nōn potestis. 2. Cum negāre posset, omnia repente confessus est. 3. Ut crīmen vērum fuisset, reus sine testibus nōn condemnandus erat. 4. Quamvīs dīligēns cōnsul esset. in senātū nōn semper aderat. 5. Quamquam causae nātiōnis externae ēloquentiā adfuit, populus bellum suscipere nōn voluērunt. 6. Jūdex famae reī nocuit, etiamsī invītus. 7. Ut īnfāmia magna esset. ab illīs jūdicibus nōn condemnandus erat. 8. Tametsī mīles fortis vulnus capitis grave nōn accēpisset, mortuus esset. 9. Quamquam cīvitās cōnservāta est, nōndum perīculō līberī sumus. 10. Quamquam ita respondit, nōndum eum in vincula conjiciam. 11. Quamquam litterae sine nōmine erant, scīvimus quis eās scrīpsisset. 12. Quamquam nox erat, Rōmam nōn rediit. 13. Quamquam suppliciō acerbō dignī erant, nihil fecit. 14. Quamquam nullus equitātus eīs erat, vīcērunt. 15. Etiamsī equitātum habuisset, nōn vīcisset. 16. Etiamsī litterae sine nōmine essent, tamen scīrem quis eās scrīpsisset. 17. Quamvīs dīvēs sīs, nōn es beātus. 18. Quamvīs bonus sīs, erunt quī tē ōderint. 19. Captī sunt quamquam cūrā ūsī sunt.

Exercise 83.—1. Quamquam jam diū in nōs machināris, tamen tē nōn timeō. 2. Etsī nōn crēdās, sciō quid proximā nocte ēgerīs. 3. Etsī audeat in senātum venīre, nōn jubeam eum comprehendī. 4. Quamquam jam diū nōs omnēs interficere cōnārīs, tamen contrā rem pūblicam tē commovēre nōn potes. 5. Etsī tē ad mortem dūcī jubeam, relīqua manus iste etiam tum vīvat. 6. Etsī improbissimus vir es, tamen īnfitiārī nōn potes tē hoc dīxisse. 7. Etsī morte dignus est, nē eum condemnēmus. 8. Nōlī interficere eum quamquam inimīcus reī pūblicae est. 9. Quamquam adsunt quī Catilīnam dēfendant, dīcō eum inimīcissimum reī pūblicae et perditissimum omnium hominum esse. 10. Quamquam eum ad mortem dūcī oportet, nōndum hoc jūbēbō. 11. Etsī mentem mutet, etiam tum odiō mihi sit. 12. Quamquam nocte convēnistis, sciō quī vōbīscum fuerint. 13. Etsī id īnfitiātus esset, eum in vincula conjēcissēmus. 14. Quamquam Catilīnam nōn comprehendit, scīvit quid factūrus esset. 15. Etsī nōnnullī eum laudārent, nōn laudārem. 16. Quamquam Rōmam mānē prōfectus est, nōn pervēnit ante noctem. 17. Sī hoc fēcistī, in vincula conjiciēris. 18. Sī vestrum est dēfendere rem pūblicam, cūr nōn dēfenditis? 19. Caesarī ingenium magnum fuerit, tamen mōrēs ējus admīrārī nōn possum. 20. Mē nōn dēfendistis, quamquam vestrum est id facere. 21. Quamquam dēnique līberī perīculō sumus, etiam nunc vestrum est mē dēfendere. 22. Etsī in senātum veniat, eum nōn comprehendam. 23. Etsī Rōmā nōn ēgrediātur, eum nōn timeāmus. 24. Quamquam dīligentissimī erant, tamen praetōrēs ā Cicerōne missī eōs cēpērunt. 25. Etsī vērum sit, nōn timeāmus. 26. Quamquam litterās ex domiciliō ējus dētulerāmus, tamen negāvit sē eās scrīpsisse.

Cicero's Letters, p. 328.—Tully to his Terentia and Daddy to his very sweet daughter, Cicero to his mother and sister—(both) send heartiest greetings.

I think you ought to consider carefully again and again, my dears, what to do. whether to remain at Rome or be with me in some safe place. This is not my problem alone, but yours too.

It occurs to me that you could safely remain in Rome under Dolabella's protection, and this arrangement would be of great advantage if there happens to be any force or plundering; but on the other hand, it disturbs me to see that all honest citizens have left Rome and taken their women with them. The territory in which I am consists both of towns under our patronage and of estates which I own, so that you could be with me frequently and, when you went abroad, would readily find yourself in our own estates.

It isn't sufficiently clear to me yet which of the two courses is preferable. See what the other women in the same situation are doing, for fear you would not be permitted to leave when you wished. I want you to think it over carefully between you again and again, and discuss it with your friends.

Have Philotimus make the house secure. Please organize special letter-carriers so that I may receive word from you daily. Take good care now to stay well, if you wish us well.

Formiae, January 27.

Lesson 21

Exercise 84.—1. Some merchants have no money because they shirk effort and exertion. (*Quia vītant*, Gr. 572.) 2. I did not wish to buy a home because I did not have enough money. (*Quod esset*, Gr. 573.) 3. The young man did not follow Christ because he had many possessions which he did not wish to sell. (*Quia habēret*, Gr. 573.) 4. I love her not because she belongs to my own race, but because she is beautiful. (*Nōn quod sit*, Gr. 574.) 5. And going into the temple, Christ cast them out because they were selling and buying in the house of prayer. (*Quoniam vēnderent, emerent*, Gr. 573.) 6. Since this is so, it is necessary to wait longer. (*Cum sint*, Gr. 578.) 7. He was glad that I did not give money to the merchants. (*Quod dedī*, Gr. 579, 2.) 8. All Christians rejoice in hope. (*Spē*, Gr. 781.) 9. He was unable to speak for pain. (*Prae dolōre*, Gr. 784.) 10. Christ was sold by a friend for the price of a slave. (*Pretiō*, Gr. 788.) 11. But Christ bought us with His own blood. (*Sanguine suō*, Gr. 788). 12. The soldiers rejoiced as if they had seen their home. (*Quasi vīdissent*, Gr. 611.) 13. You speak with me as if I were the accused. (*Quasi essem*, Gr. 612.) 14. We ought to regard true friends very highly. (*Permagnī*, Gr. 701.) 15. Many things which I formerly valued very highly, I hold less highly now. (*Maximī*, Gr. 701.) 16. I don't consider men of this sort worth anything. (*Nihilī*, Gr. 702.) 17. Since these things were discovered in the Senate, I will explain them all to you. (*Quoniam comperta sunt*, Gr. 572.) 18. It is worth it if you leave the city. (*Tantī*, Gr. 700.) 19. Saints think very little of honor.

(*Parvī*, Gr. 701.) 20. He praised the praetors for having undertaken the task without delay. (*Laudāvit suscēpissent*, Gr. 576.) 21. Since this is so, we ought to cast him into prison. (*Cum sint*, Gr. 578.) 22. Since we see all these beautiful things, should we not affirm that there is a God? (*Cum videāmus*, Gr. 578.) 23. Rejoicing in this triumph, he went to Rome. (*Hāc victōriā*, Gr. 781.) 24. The victory cost considerable bloodshed. (*Sanguine*, Gr. 788.) 25. Go to your homes, for it is now night. (*Quoniam est*, Gr. 572.) 26. I am glad you have conquered the enemy. (*Quod subēgistī*, Gr. 579, 2.) 27. My friend is the same as he always was. (*Īdem quī*, Gr. 608.)

Exercise 85.—1. Mercātōrēs victōriā gāvīsī sunt. 2. Multō sanguine constābat, sed tantī erat. 3. Quoniam jam est nox, domōs vestrās ab industriā vestrā discēdite. 4. Nōs omnēs Chrīstus ēmit carō pretiō sanguinis suī. 5. Hī mercātōrēs Rōmānī pecūniam multam habent quoniam bona vilī pretiō emunt et carō pretiō vēndunt. 6. Trēs rēgēs conspectū Jesūs et Marīae gāvīsī sunt. 7. Sunt quī Deum ament nōn quod bonus in sē est sed quod in perpetuum condemnārī nōlunt. 8. Complūra quae anteā maximī aestimāvī, nunc nihilī putō. 9. Necesse est et sē et suam ipsīus patriam industriā ac labōre dēfendere. 10. Omnēs difficultātēs industriā superantur. 11. Sunt quī genera externa ōderint quasi hostēs sint. 12. Industriā ac labōre cōnsulis conservātī sumus quasi nullum perīculum obīissēmus. 13. Quoniam rēs pūblica servāta est, grātiae Deō ā nōbīs agendae sunt. 14. Haec victōria multō sanguine constābat. 15. Cum ita responderit, eum in vincula conjiciēmus. 16. Quia litterae sine nōmine erant, nescīvimus quis eās scrīpsisset. 17. Cum jam nox sit, Rōmam revertī debēmus. 18. Honōrem parvī facit. 19. Populus hāc victōriā gāvīsus est. 20. Mīlitēs laudāvit quod urbem dēfendissent. 21. Acerbiōre suppliciō dignī sunt quia cīvibus suīs īnsidiātī sunt. 22. Guadeō quod vēnistī. 23. Minōris est. 24. Victī sunt quia equitātum nōn habuērunt. 25. Pecūniae causā et propter amōrem patriae, Rōmae vīvere voluit. 26. Dolor per tōtam urbem erat quod Cicerō interfectus erat. 27. Rōmānī flōruērunt quia fortēs erant. 28. Per tōtam urbem erant corpora eōrum quī occisī erant. 29. Tē jam diū timēmus, cum sciāmus tē voluisse urbem incendere et cīvēs interficere.

Exercise 86.—1. Litterae sine nōmine erant. 2. Gallia male pācāta est. 3. Dīxit contrōversiam dē hāc rē fuisse. 4. Ōrāvit eōs ut sē dēfenderent. 5. Dīxit sē imāginum bonārum semper studiōsum fuisse. 6. Erat eī mens natūrā ad facinus apta. 7. Ut levissimē dīcam, adjuvāre nōs nōluērunt. 8. Hortātus est ut sine timōre loquerentur. 9. Omnēs scientiā dīcendī superat. 10. Litterās cognōvērunt. 11. Tantī est. 12. Eum parvī putō. 13. Patent portae. 14. Utinam Cicerō nē mortuus esset. 15. Prōvidēbunt ut in perpetuā pāce sint. 16. Comperit omnia vēra esse. 17. Nōs vincere potuērunt. 18. Nūtū Deī īnsidiae compertae sunt. 19. Rēs pūblicae ē maximīs perīculīs ērepta est. 20. Jam nox est. 21. Ad vestra tecta discēdite. 22. Multa aliēna bella gessit. 23. Omnēs impetūs cīvium malōrum in mē ūnum conversī sunt. 24. Utinam vēnissēs. 25. Tē iterum videam. 26. Invidiam in administrandā rē pūblicā suscēpī. 27. Ad glōriam meam valeat. 28. Rem pūblicam semper dēfendās. 29. Reprehendit eōs quod rem pūblicam nōn dēfendissent. 30. Veniant. 31. Hī virī vōcem conscientiae neglēxērunt. 32. Eōrum facta eīs prōfuērunt. 33. Tibi prōvidendum est nē occīdar. 34. Vestrum est mē līberōsque meōs dēfendere. 35. Litterae erant in eandem ferē sententiam. 36. Mihi jam nocēre nōn possunt. 37. Rōmam aliquandō videam. 38. Dīxit eōs ventūrōs esse. 39. Arbitrātus sum ceterōs exitūrōs esse. 40. Rogāvērunt nōs ut sē adjuvārēmus. 41. Cicerō Rōmānōs rogāvit ut sē ipsum dēfenderent. 42. Rēs pūblica tacita rogat ut sē dēfendātis. 43. Utinam nē captus essēs. 44. Utinam Rōmae essēs. 45. Dīxit haec virtūte nōn cāsū gesta esse. 46. Hortātus est ut cōnfiterentur. 47. Prōvidēbō nē hoc vōbīs diū faciendum sit. 48. In perpetuā pāce erant. 49. Cum jam nox sit, in vestra tecta discēdite. 50. Deō grātiās agere dēbēmus.

Exercise 87.—Diēs noctēsque in hōc labōre cōnsūmpsī ut in perpetuā pāce esse possītis. Semper arbitrātus sum bonī cōnsulis esse prōvidēre ut cīvēs perīculō et metū līberī sint. Quoniam eōrum quī in rē pūblica versantur nōn eadem est fortūna atque condiciō quae illōrum quī in litterīs versantur, quod contrā illōs impetūs impiōrum ac nefāriōrum hominum vertuntur, hōrum autem scrīpta solum ā bonīs leguntur et ā malīs negleguntur, vestrum est—sī mihi jūre ac meritō est certa spēs laudis et glōriae—dēfendere nōmen meum atque factum meum contrā hostēs hūjus urbis et vestrōs. In vōbīs, cīvēs, meam spem salūtis et perpetuae laudis pōnō.

Cicero's Training in Oratory, p. 336.—I was with Diodotus the Stoic, who recently died in my home, as he had been dwelling in my house and living with me. I had devoted myself to this teacher and to his many different arts, but nevertheless so that no day went by without exercises in oratorical techniques.

I used to practice declamation, as they say now, with Marcus Piso and Quintus Pompey or someone else daily; I was doing much of it in Latin, but more often in Greek, partly because a Greek speech, supplying as it did more rhetorical ornaments, offered practice in speaking

Latin similarly, and partly because without speaking in Greek I could neither be corrected nor taught by the Greek masters.

At that time we first began to attend both private and public cases, in order not to learn in the Forum as many did, but to go into the Forum as well trained as we were able to make ourselves. At the same time I studied under Molo, who had come to Rome as an envoy about the claims of the people of Rhodes when Sulla was dictator. And so my first public case, that in behalf of Sextus Roscius, received so much commendation it seemed there would not be any case that could not fittingly be entrusted to my defense.

I had at that time great slenderness and weakness of body, and a long thin neck, and this appearance and figure is considered not far from being perilous to life if combined with effort and severe strain on the lungs; and this disturbed those who loved me the more because I spoke without relaxing, without any change in my manner of delivery, with the strongest possible voice and with exertion of the whole body. And so although both my friends and the doctors begged me to stop taking cases, I thought I should rather undergo any danger at all rather than give up the hoped-for oratorical fame. But when I realized that with relaxation and moderation of voice and by a changed style of speaking, I could avoid the danger and speak more restrainedly, this induced me to set out for Asia Minor, where I could change my manner of speaking.

And so it was that after two years' experience in defense cases and when my name was already well known in the Forum I left Rome. Arriving in Athens, I again took up the study of philosophy, the continuous cultivation and enrichment of which I had never interrupted since early youth. Afterward I traversed all Asia Minor and stayed with the greatest orators, and with their good will practiced under them.

Not content with these masters, I went to Rhodes, and attached myself to that same Molo whom I had heard at Rome, since he was at the time pleader for real cases and an outstanding writer, and most judicious in marking out and calling attention to faults and in instructing and teaching. He took care as well as he could to restrain from liberty and license our youthful flood of words that was brimming and flowing over and to confine within bounds the speech that overflowed its banks. Thus I returned after a two-year period not only better trained, but quite changed; for I had overcome the habit of excessive vocal strain, my speech had as it were cooled off, and I had gained strength of lungs and attained a more medium build.

General Review Exercises

Exercise 88.—1. Quamquam vītās et fortūnās vestrās servāvimus, adhuc paulum perīculī est. 2. Omnēs interitū servātī estis maximō auxiliō deōrum immortālium. 3. Operā et cōnsiliō meō morte ipsā ēreptī estis. 4. Sī vīta nōbīs cārior est omnibus aliīs rēbus, nōnne dēbēmus laudāre Cicerōnem quod nōs exitiō et interitū servāverit? 5. Rogāvit num cōnsilia cōnjūrātōrum omnibus bonīs nōn manifesta essent. 6. Quis nōn laudet Cicerōnem quod Catilīnam virum perniciōsum ad mortem dūcerit? 7. Cīvis fuerit, tamen inimīcus reī pūblicae erat. 8. Vōbīs expōnam quōmodo hīc rē pūblicae hostis captus sit. 9. Nōnne Cicerō in honōre apud omnēs hominēs habērī dēbet? 10. Nōnne Catilīna paucīs ante diēbus ex urbe ēgressus est?

Exercise 89.—1. Quamquam litterae praetōribus trāditae sunt, eās nōn lēgērunt. 2. Nisi eōs tum convocāvissem, ex urbe fūgissent. 3. Quamquam signum cognōvit, cōnfiterī nōluit. 4. Ipse Cicerō litterās nōn lēgit. 5. Cicerōnem laudāvērunt quod eās nōn lēgisset. 6. Accidit ut multī et illustrēs virī paucīs horīs domum Cicerōnis venīrent. 7. Utinam istās litterās numquam scrīpsissent! 8. Sulpicium mīsī quī vidēret quid tēlōrum in domiciliō Cethēgī esset. 9. Quamquam multa tēla in domiciliō ējus inventa sunt, negāvit sē inimīcum reī pūblicae esse. 10. "Semper," inquit, "bonōrum tēlōrum studiōsus fuī."

Exercise 90.—1. Catilīna ex urbe ējiciendus est. 2. Quamquam hī virī Rōmae erant, nōndum ausus sum imperāre ut in vincula conjicerentur. 3. Rōmae erant quī nescīrent quid cōnsiliī hī caperent. 4. Rem ita expōnere voluī ut īnsidiās hostium oculīs vestrīs vidērētis. 5. Diēs noctēsque cōnsūmpsī ut salūtī vestrae prōvidērem. 6. Voluī tōtam rem intellegī nōn sōlum ā mē ipsō, nōn sōlum ā senātū, sed etiam ā vōbīs. 7. Dīxit eōs negōtium sine morā suscēpisse. 8. Flaccum, virum optimum, mīsit quī Gallōs caperet. 9. Quis Cicerōnem reprehendat quod fēcerit ea quae fēcit? 10. Laus et glōria Cicerōnī cāriōrēs erant pecūniā vel etiam vītā ipsā.

Exercise 91.—1. Hortātus sum eōs ut līberē loquerentur. 2. Rogāvī eōs quid dē rē scīrent. 3. Catilīna imperāverat eī ut ad urbem cum servīs paucīs diēbus venīret. 4. Omnēs Catilīnae amīcī Cicerōnem pertimuērunt. 5. Catilīna dīxerat urbem incendendam esse. 6. Jusserat eōs interficere omnēs cīvēs quī eīs restitērunt. 7. "Lentulus," inquiunt Gallī, "nōbīs litterās et pecūniam prō vestrā gente dedit. Dīxit sē factūrum esse nōs omnēs cīvēs. Ille īdem dīxit sē fātō esse quī imperium tōtīus urbis cunctaeque Italiae obtinēret." 8. Cicerōnem laudāvērunt quod sē metū līberāvisset atque vītās et fortūnās suās servāvisset. 9. Equitātus Gallōrum melior fuit quam Rōmānōrum. 10. Quamquam nōnnullī urbem vastāre noluērunt, Catilīna dīxit eam incendendam esse.

Exercise 92.—1. Pollicitus est sē factūrum esse omnia quae vellent. 2. Fortis fuerit! Doctus fuerit! Quid inde? 3. Cicerō eum rogāvit num signum cognōsceret. 4. "Certē," inquit, "est imāgō avī meī. Num hōrum crīminum condemnandus sum quia nesciōquis signō meō ūsus est?" 5. Quamquam prīmum omnia negāvit, tandem cōnfessus est et in vincula conjectus est. 6. Cūrā ut vir sīs. Cūrā ut auxilium etiam servōrum ad tē conjungās. 7. Quamquam litterās ē domō ējus dētulerat, hīc tamen negāvit sē eās scrīpsisse.

Exercise 93.—Nōnne, patrēs cōnscriptī, certissima indicia criminis eōrum nōbīs sunt? Revocāte in animās vestrās litterās, signa, manum. Revocāte verba ipsōrum et Gallōrum. Diēs noctēsque cōnsūmpsī ut haec omnia manifesta vōbīs essent. Quis eōs perniciōsōs cīvēs nōn condemnet? Quis eōrum morte rem pūblicam perīculō et metū nōn līberet? Num in hōc conventū possunt esse quī Catilīnam, virum perniciōsissimum, Lentulum, virum nefārium, Cethēgum, reī pūblicam pestem, nōn ōderint ac timeant? Sint cīvēs; quis nōn arbitrētur eōs hostēs reī pūblicae potius quam amantēs cīvitātis? Patria, ut ita dīcam, eōs jam diū dēfendit ac colit; quam istī odiō habuērunt, et jam diū illud tantum cupiunt: istam patriam exstinguere, tecta omnium nostrum atque adeō templa deōrum immortālium incendere.